The Fiscal Affairs Department

Understanding Revenue Administration

Results from the Second Survey of the Revenue Administration – Fiscal Information Tool

Duncan Cleary, William Crandall, and Andrew Masters

INTERNATIONAL MONETARY FUND

Cataloging-in-Publication Data

Joint Bank-Fund Library

Names: International Monetary Fund. Fiscal Affairs Department.
Title: Understanding revenue administration : results from the second survey of the Revenue Administration :
   fiscal information tool.
Description: Washington, DC : International Monetary Fund, [2017] | At head of title: The Fiscal Affairs
   Department. | Includes bibliographical references.

Identifiers: ISBN 9781484301913 (paper)

Subjects: LCSH: Revenue management | Tax administration and procedure.

Classification: LCC HD60.7.U526 2017

Publication orders may be placed online, by fax, or through the mail:
International Monetary Fund, Publication Services
P.O. Box 92780, Washington, DC 20090, U.S.A.
Tel. (202) 623-7430 Fax: (202) 623-7201
E-mail: publications@imf.org
www.imfbookstore.org
www.elibrary.imf.org

Contents

Figures

Tables

Appendix Tables

Acknowledgments

This paper presents the results of the second round of the **Revenue Administration Fiscal Information Tool (RA-FIT)**. It is made possible by the participation of IMF member countries that provided data. This round was a joint venture with the Inter-American Center of Tax Administrations. The authors are members of the RA-FIT team, based in the Fiscal Affairs Department (FAD) of the IMF. Staff in the revenue administration divisions and in the IMF's Regional Technical Assistance Centers were most helpful in conducting the survey.

The authors' views as expressed in this paper do not necessarily reflect the views of FAD. Errors and omissions are the authors' sole responsibility. Summary information presented in this paper is derived from data that are self-reported by participants and thus may be subject to review and change without prior notice; this is particularly true for data maintained on the RA-FIT Data Portal.

Funding for the RA-FIT project was provided by the IMF and by the Tax Policy and Administration Topical Trust Fund (TPA-TTF); both sources are gratefully acknowledged. The following donor governments and organizations contribute to the TPA-TTF: the Africa, Caribbean and Pacific Group of States; Belgium; the European Union; Germany; the Republic of Korea; Kuwait; Luxembourg; the Netherlands; Norway; and Switzerland.

Additional documentation, data, and information are available online through the RA-FIT Data Portal at http://data.rafit.org.

Executive Summary

This paper presents the results of the second round of the **Revenue Administration Fiscal Information Tool (RA-FIT)** country survey in an aggregated manner for all respondents and by income group. Notwithstanding regional biases and some data quality issues with the sample, broad insights and trends are discernable from the data, and the results form part of an evolving series that will continue to develop and grow with the **International Survey On Revenue Administration (ISORA)**, the successor survey to RA-FIT conducted by the IMF in collaboration with the Inter-American Center of Tax Administrations (CIAT), the Intra-European Organisation of Tax Administration (IOTA), and the Organisation for Economic Co-operation and Development (OECD). This paper expands on a previous one, which covered the first round of RA-FIT (Lemgruber and others 2015),[1] and aims to allow countries to access information about key measures in revenue administration. Unlike the first paper, this one does not cover issues specific to customs administration but focuses rather on tax administration data.

There were 89 participants, with an average completion rate across the survey of 81 percent. The participants were mainly from Latin America, sub-Saharan Africa, the Caribbean, and the Pacific region, with a smaller contingent from Europe and the Middle East. Thus, there is a bias toward the Southern Hemisphere in the data.

Institutional Arrangements: The respondents represent a wide range of governance structure models. Forty-five percent report having a semi-autonomous status, in which tax and customs are typically managed in an inte-

---

[1]Available under the publication tab in the RA-FIT Data Portal: http://data.rafit. org/?sk=3dba84d7-1dd8-4533-b682-c0dfcb1d7f13&sId=1445908451587

grated[2] manner within the same administration. These semi-autonomous organizations appear to show greater autonomy and transparency across a range of measured areas than those that do not classify themselves as being semi-autonomous.

Staff and Offices: The mix of staff types varies across income groups, and as income levels increase, it seems that proportionately more staff are assigned to audit and investigations functions.

Taxpayer Segmentation and Registration: The majority of respondents across all income levels have a large taxpayer office (LTO) or unit (over 84 percent) and some sort of regime for small taxpayers. The most common means of assigning taxpayers to either taxpayer segment is based on turnover. The majority (over 90 percent) also have a value-added tax (VAT). Data were also sought on the major tax types, such as corporate and personal income taxes (CIT and PIT). In spite of the importance of an accurate and reliable register, a large number of respondents across income groups had difficulty providing high-quality responses regarding the activity status of their registered taxpayers; that is, whether taxpayers are considered active or inactive.

Taxpayer Return Filing: On-time filing rates vary across tax, time, and income levels. VAT tends to have the best results at about 70 percent. Key income taxes (for example, CIT and PIT) have lower on-time filing rates at, on average, 50 percent to 60 percent. This seems lower than expected and suggests considerable room for improvement. In some cases, the rates may be tied to inaccurate register data on active taxpayers, which would inflate the number of expected returns. Some administrations show improved filing rates at a point six months from the due date, but this is far from universal.

Taxpayer Service: Taxpayers communicate with their administrations via a number of contact channels; the most commonly used channel by the surveyed group (averaging over 46 percent) is in-person or face-to-face communication. This is a costly channel to maintain compared with other channels and again suggests some room for change. Other channels used were telephone (27 percent), hardcopy correspondence (letters) (16 percent), and electronic correspondence (email/Internet) (11 percent).

Arrears, Verification, and Disputes: Response rates to questions on these critically important areas were among the lowest in the survey. Arrears increased in the years surveyed, albeit with some slowing in the rate of increase for lower-income countries. Audits are still mostly comprehensive in lower-income countries (50 percent of intervention types), suggesting that

---

[2]In this context, "integrated" usually does not mean that tax and customs administrations are entirely integrated but that they are separate branches reporting to a single head of administration.

scope exists for the use of other, less costly, intervention types. Little data were provided on disputes or appeals, suggesting a gap in many administrations' performance management information capabilities in this area. These data are at the core of compliance management, so the fact that many countries cannot provide them suggests that compliance monitoring is weak in those countries.

1 Introduction

RA-FIT is a survey-based data-gathering initiative designed to collect revenue administration information. The data gathered include both quantitative and qualitative information and encompass a mixture of baseline and profile data, inputs, and performance-related data. Information is provided online by IMF member countries or countries supported by IMF Regional Technical Assistance Centers (RTACs). These data have multiple purposes and multiple users, including the countries themselves.

The following are the key objectives of RA-FIT:

- Elevate the importance of revenue administration performance reporting and measurement globally.
- Gather data across a large number of tax and customs administrations to permit further analytical work, such as
  - Understanding historical performance,
  - Establishing baselines by income group and other groupings,
  - Identifying trends,
  - Flagging policy and administrative inefficiencies,
  - Refining performance measures to improve robustness, and
  - Providing sufficient data to facilitate focused and in-depth research.

- Assist in developing international revenue administration performance measurements and reporting standards.
- Improve the quality of revenue administration technical assistance.
- Provide necessary data to better calibrate other tools, such as the Tax Administration Diagnostic Assessment Tool (TADAT).

- Make data and analyses available to member countries to enable them to monitor their performance and benchmark themselves vis-à-vis other countries.
- Establish baseline measures (key performance indicators) for the technical assistance programs of all providers and provide a more detailed data source for a results-based management framework.

The first round of RA-FIT was piloted in 2012 and was the beginning of an iterative process designed to continuously improve the RA-FIT survey over time. One by-product of the Round 1 data was the publication in 2015 of "Understanding Revenue Administration" (Lemgruber and others 2015), an initial data analysis (for 2010) using the data gathered by RA-FIT. As a result of the Round 1 experience, many improvements were incorporated into Round 2, which commenced in May 2014 on a Web-based platform. This paper presents Round 2 data (for 2011, 2012, and 2013) on an aggregated basis and offers further preliminary analysis and observations on a number of related topics.

Response rates for questions are set out in Table 1. Responses are grouped by income group.[1] The majority of countries from Round 1 also participated in Round 2, but some did not, and there were some new countries as well. Some important characteristics of the respondents that were noted for Round 1 also apply for Round 2 in that many of the administrations: (1) are comprised of less-mature organizations; (2) have poor management information systems; and (3) have significant capacity constraints. The RA-FIT initiative continues to highlight the urgent need to improve the development of performance measurement and management in the respondent countries.

Table 1. Response Rates for Tax Administration by Income Group

	LIC	LMIC	UMIC	HIC	Total
Round 1	20	29	26	6	**81**
Round 2	21	28	29	11	**89**

Source: RA-FIT databases for Rounds 1 and 2.

All data presented in this document are aggregated based on survey responses or information derived from them. Participating countries will have access to the individual responses of other participants but may not make that data

---

[1] Economies are divided according to 2012 gross national income per capita, calculated using the World Bank Atlas method. The groups are low-income countries (LICs), $1,035 or less; lower-middle-income countries (LMICs), $1,036 to $4,085; upper-middle-income countries (UMICs), $4,086 to $12,615; and high-income countries (HICs), $12,616 or more.

public in any way without the permission of the country concerned. Aggregated data are presented only where the sample size is at least five countries.

One major reason for collecting revenue administration performance and other information (usually through surveys) is to help senior executives of revenue administrations manage and evaluate their administrations. Various international organizations have been collecting such information for some time: the Inter-American Center of Tax Administrations, the IMF, the Intra-European Organisation of Tax Administrations, and the Organisation for Economic Co-operation and Development.

The OECD has published a comprehensive comparative information series on tax administration since 2004. It uses data collected in a biannual survey that currently includes 34 OECD countries and 22 non-OECD countries. IOTA gathers data regularly from its members for internal analysis and review. CIAT in 2011 published comprehensive tax administration data on many Latin American countries and intends to continue doing so. The IMF, for its part, has been collecting tax and customs data since 2012 through RA-FIT. For 2016, a broadened partnership of the four international organizations (CIAT, IMF, IOTA, OECD) agreed to collect tax administration performance data and other information using a common survey to be known as the **International Survey on Revenue Administration**. But although there will be a single data collection survey, the organizations will continue to produce their own analyses and contextualization of the data in a manner that best meets the needs of their members.

There will be immediate benefits for administrations participating in ISORA:

- Countries that are members of more than one of these organizations need provide data and statistical information only once.
- There will be a common platform for collection—the Web-based data collection platform developed for RA-FIT.
- There will be a single, seamless survey on an annual basis (ISORA), using common questions and definitions.

There will also be longer-term benefits for participating administrations and for international organizations, primarily the following:

- A larger database for better analysis, using trends and advanced analytical techniques.
- Improved ability to identify inefficiencies and diagnose problems.
- The development of inputs that can be used to assist in determining and improving benchmarks; for example, in TADAT.

- The compilation of baseline and profile data, both quantitative and qualitative, that can lead to improvements in efficiency and effectiveness.

2 The RA-FIT Round 2 Survey

For effective performance management, both within and among organizations, basic data are required to measure performance and to understand the context within which revenue administrations are performing. Gathering and providing analyses of the RA-FIT data will help revenue administrations improve their focus on performance management, provide data to facilitate analyses and technical assistance, and allow cross-country comparisons to be made on revenue administration over a range of indicators where this has not previously been possible. Trends and changes over time can also be reviewed within administrations, within and among groups, and at the overall level. Round 2 of RA-FIT should be seen as part of a continuing effort to improve performance management in revenue administration; this effort is entering a new phase with the initiation of the International Survey on Revenue Administration.

RA-FIT Round 2 Survey

The RA-FIT Round 2 survey consisted of a number of forms geared to capture key data on revenue administration. The forms were assigned depending on whether the respondent was a revenue (tax and customs) administration or a tax administration. Table 2 lists the forms used in Round 2.

The Round 2 survey was conducted in partnership with the Inter-American Center of Tax Administrations. CIAT respondents were required to complete additional questions in a number of forms to satisfy that institution's requirements, and these are not covered in this publication.

The period covered by Round 2 is from 2011 to 2013. This builds on Round 1, for which 2010 provided the most comprehensive data set. While many similarities exist between the questions in Rounds 1 and 2, they do not

Table 2. Round 2 Forms Used

Tax and Customs	Tax Only
1. Revenue Statistics	4. Taxpayer Segmentation
2. Institutional Arrangements	5. Taxpayer Registration
3. Staffing and Office Network	6. Return Filing
	7. Taxpayer Services
	8. Arrears
	9. Verification/Audit
	10. Dispute Resolution

always map directly, as a number of revisions were made in the Round 2 survey, including an expansion of some of the forms.

RA-FIT Round 2 Forms

Details of the forms used in Round 2 are as follows.[1]

Revenue Statistics

This first form seeks details of total revenues collected across all tax types, as well as customs duties, excise revenue, and nontax revenue where applicable. These data were provided in local currency, and computations regarding distribution of total revenue and each distribution as a percentage of GDP were made within the form as data were entered and saved. The form also contains questions on estimating tax expenditures. Some of the revenue data, such as cost of collection, are used to calculate other derived indicators in other forms.

Institutional Arrangements

This form covers aspects of administration such as framework, tax and customs integration, management boards, degree of autonomy, reporting activity and transparency, accountability, outsourcing of services, IT solutions, and details of the administration's budget. Many of these questions have a binary response (Yes/No). The questions allow for an understanding not only of the range and types of administrations but also of the relationships between these frameworks and performance measures.

---

[1]Forms are available in PDF format on the RA-FIT Data Portal: http://data.rafit. org/?sk=3dba84d7-1dd8-4533-b682-c0dfcb1d7f13&sId=1445908451587

Staffing and Office Network

This form covers details of staff and office numbers and functions in operations and other areas in the administrations, captured at the FTE (full-time equivalent) level.

Taxpayer Segmentation

This form seeks information regarding the operations of LTOs and simplified regimes for small taxpayers. The data have been used to establish baselines and allow for comparisons with general operations and among administrations.

Taxpayer Registration

This form covers aspects of aspects of registration across Income taxes (CIT, PIT, PAYE) VAT, sales tax and excise.

Return Filing/VAT Return Filing

This form collects information on return filing/VAT return filing, including thresholds for registration. It also covers aspects of return filing across the major taxes (CIT, PIT, PAYE, VAT, and sales tax), including on-time filing rates. In the online platform, VAT was presented as a separate form for design purposes, but in this publication the results for filing are presented together. The VAT section also covers the type of return filed; that is, credit, debit, or nil returns.

Taxpayer Services

This form seeks information on the contact channels used by taxpayers and the volumes and relative proportions of contact events.

Tax Arrears

This form deals with the stock and flow of arrears over the fiscal years covered by Round 2.

Verification/Audit

This form gathers data on the types of intervention carried out by administrations and the resulting assessment values, with a subset dealing with results for large taxpayers.

Dispute Resolution

This form covers results of administrative reviews of disputes (objections) and details of the age and results of litigation (appeals) in both volume and value.

Response Rate and Sample for Round 2

Eighty-nine countries (of 112 invited) provided responses in Round 2 of RA-FIT. This was an increase over Round 1, which had 81 responses. Many countries that participated in Round 1 also participated in Round 2 (66 of

Figure 1. Geographic Distribution of Round 2 Respondents

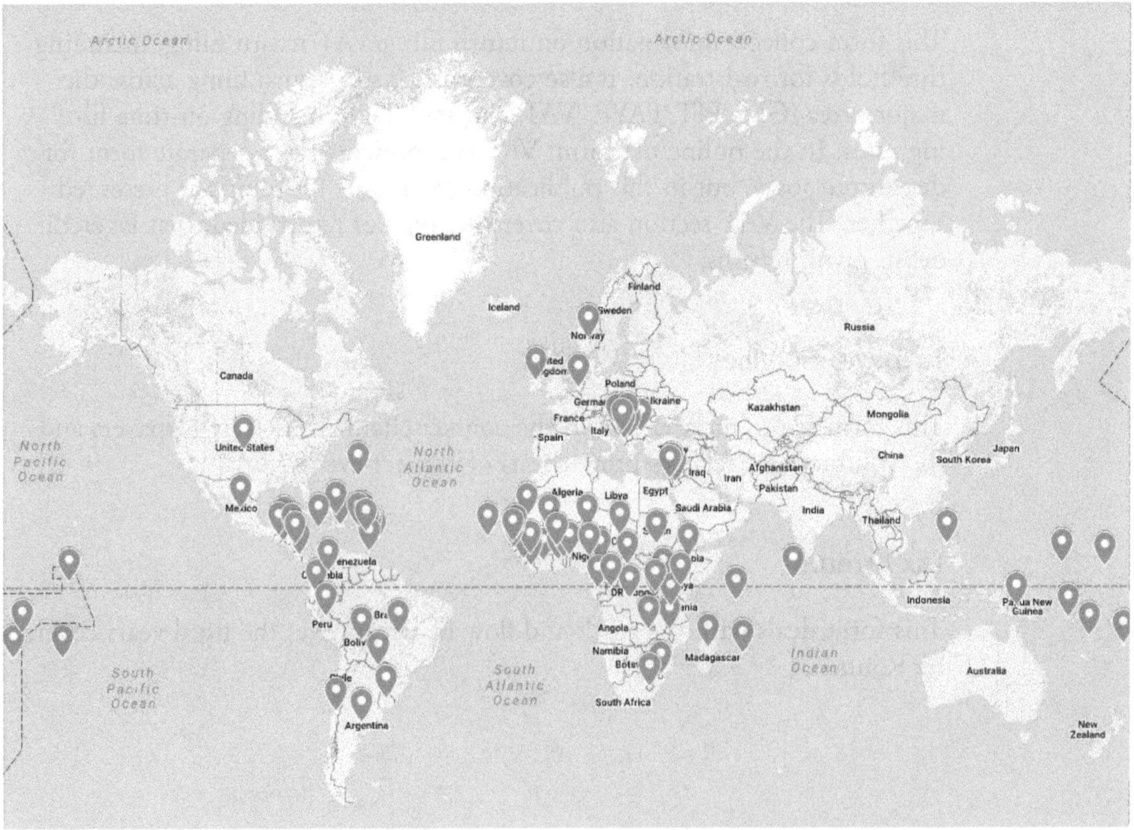

the 89, or about 74 percent). Partnering with CIAT ensured high participation among its members in Latin America. The data contain a bias toward the Southern Hemisphere, reflecting focus areas of IMF technical assistance delivery and the presence of RTACs in certain central locations.[2] Figure 1 summarizes the geographic distribution of the participants. This will change with Round 3 and ISORA, especially by adding members of the OECD Forum for Tax Administration and of IOTA.

Overall, the average completion rate across forms for tax respondents was 81 percent. High completion rates were achieved on average across all the forms, but the average rate did decrease toward the end of the survey, as illustrated in Figure 2.

Figure 2. Average Completion Rates per Form in Round 2

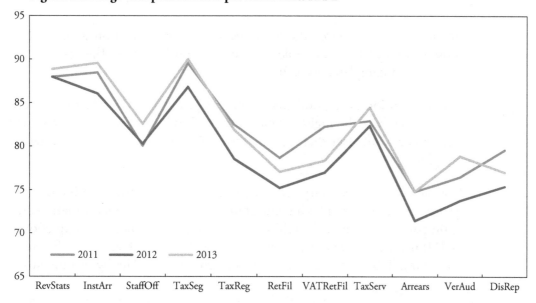

	Rev Stats	Inst Arr	Staff Off	Tax Seg	Tax Reg	Ret Fil	VAT Ret Fil	Tax Serv	Arrears	Ver Aud	Dis Rep
	%	%	%	%	%	%	%	%	%	%	%
2011	87.9	88.4	80.0	89.5	82.4	78.6	82.2	82.9	74.7	76.4	79.5
2012	87.9	86.0	80.2	86.8	78.5	75.2	76.9	82.3	71.2	73.7	75.3
2013	88.8	89.5	82.5	89.9	81.8	77.0	78.3	84.4	74.8	78.8	77.0

[2]The IMF has nine RTACs: one in the Caribbean (CARTAC); one in Central America, including the Dominican Republic (CAPTAC-DR); five in Africa (AFRITAC Central, East, South, West, and West2); one in the Middle East (METAC); and one in the Pacific (PFTAC).

Figure 3. Sample Distribution by Income Group and Region

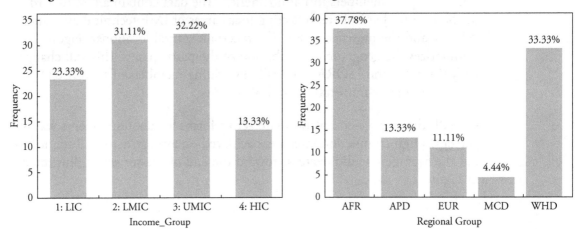

The forms that presented the most challenges for completion were similar to those in Round 1; for example, Tax Arrears and Disputes. The best year for general data completeness is 2013.

The distribution of respondents by income group and IMF region is uneven. The sample from the high-income country (HIC) category is relatively small. This is tied to the fact that Africa and the Western Hemisphere dominate the sample.

Completion rates also vary across these categories. Considering income groups, the upper-middle-income countries (UMICs) tended to fare best, again partly because of the CIAT partnership, with a median completion rate of 100 percent, while other groups had a wide range of success in finishing the survey. Table 3 provides overall form completion data by income group.

Table 3. Overall Form Completion Rate Data by Income Group

Income Group	Number of Observations	Mean	Standard Deviation	Minimum	Maximum	Median
LICs	21	83.07	24.26	18.36	100	91.88
LMICS	28	78.73	28.54	7.15	100	90.53
UMICs	29	87.06	24.55	12.76	100	100.00
HICs	12	67.68	41.18	6.06	100	97.03

Figure 4. Overall Form Completion Rate Data by Income Group

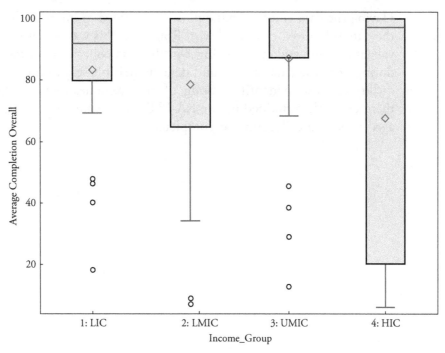

Data Quality and Data Preparation

Data

The Round 2 data set consists of a number of types of data across a wide range of topics. Numeric data include currency amounts in local currency, frequency/counting data, and percentage data. Categorical data were also captured in the form of binary response questions (Yes/No) and nominal variables, which were either dropdown single response or multi-choice radio buttons. Free text was captured for a small number of questions requiring descriptive responses, along with optional comments for each form. These comments were extensive in some cases, with caveats regarding the raw data that had been provided by respondents. Raw data were used to calculate derived data within forms once they were saved. Typically, these derived variables were totals and percentages. There are approximately 600 variables in the basic Round 2 data set. In addition, multiple derived variables (primarily ratios and percentages) were created for the purposes of analysis.

Data Quality

Having the data entered online provided options to improve the quality of the data submitted compared with Round 1. This was achieved by using validation rules and error messages in the data collection platform. However, during both the data capture and data analysis phases, a number of data quality issues were identified. Some of these were dealt with by the countries themselves when notified by the RA-FIT team, while others had to be managed after data collection was completed.

3 Institutional Arrangements

This section of the publication deals with the governance structures of revenue administrations, autonomy, transparency, capital and operating budgets, outsourcing, and Information Technology (IT) arrangements (see Appendix Tables 1 through 8).

Governance Structures

There are two common models for revenue (tax and customs) administration: (1) organizations composed of single or multiple directorates that are part of the ministry of finance, and (2) semi-autonomous organizations, with or without a management board. In addition, there are two basic types of revenue administration in terms of scope of responsibilities: (1) those in which tax and customs are separate organizational entities, and (2) those in which tax and customs are integrated to some degree. For 2013, the situation for RA-FIT Round 2 respondents is shown in Table 4.

Table 4. RA-FIT: Governance Structures for Revenue Administration

2013	Ministry Structure		Semi-autonomous Structure		Total Respondents
	No.	%	No.	%	
Tax administration only	39	76	12	24	51
Tax and customs administration	10	26	28	74	38
Total respondents	49	55	40	45	89

(Includes respondents who may not have answered this question; such respondents were assigned to a category using knowledge gleaned from other sources.)

Responses to questions are not evidence based in the same way that TADAT conclusions must be. The respondents simply present data supplied by the administration. As for whether the organization is semi-autonomous or not, respondents express their opinion on the basis of the definition given. In RA-FIT Round 1, some 40 percent of countries indicated a semi-autonomous status, with or without a management board. In Round 2, the comparable figure is 45 percent. There are many variations of the semi-autonomous model, including a formal revenue authority (with separate legislation and a management board), which is most common but which itself has a number of variations. From the data provided, it is clear that for tax administration–only organizations the likelihood of a semi-autonomous structure is only 24 percent, while for organizations in which tax and customs are integrated the likelihood of a semi-autonomous structure is significantly higher at 74 percent.

Management Boards

RA-FIT seeks a limited amount of information about management boards for revenue administrations. However, such boards are a common occurrence. In 2013, 45 percent of respondents (34) self-identified as having a semi-autonomous governance structure, with 62 percent of those (23) having a management board. In other words, 28 percent of all respondents operate with a management board of some kind. The average number of board members is eight, and half of them are from the private sector.

Most of these boards have a unique operating environment compared with other public or private sector boards: They are excluded from any involvement in specific operations (casework), hence the name *management* board. These boards appear to be more streamlined and less top-heavy than some of their counterparts. For example, in the not-for-profit sector in the United States, the average size of a management or governing board is 16.2 members (BoardSource 2012).[1] In addition, with an average of four private sector members (the other four often being ex officio, such as senior government officials) there appears to be a solid foundation for bringing private sector expertise and ideas into the revenue administration, which is one of the stated goals of many of these boards.

---

[1]From a 2012 survey by Board Source, a national organization focused on U.S. nonprofit organizations and boards.

Figure 5. Autonomy Responses Yes Rate per Question, 2013

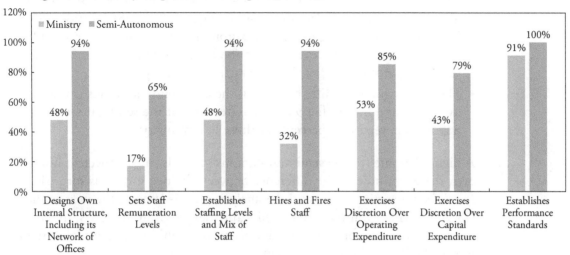

Autonomy

In the quest to increase efficiency, effectiveness, and economy in government, and to deliver services and enforce laws in a rapidly changing environment, there has been a general tendency over several decades to increase autonomy for government organizations. The basic principle is that such autonomy can lead to better performance by removing impediments to effective and efficient management while maintaining appropriate accountability and transparency (IMF 2010). In the context of revenue administration, autonomy refers to the degree to which the administration is able to operate independently from government in terms of legal form and status; funding and budget; and financial, human resources and administrative practices.

RA-FIT asks seven key Yes/No questions related to autonomy: four in the field of human resources, two related to budget, and one dealing with performance management. Overall, for 2013, survey respondents had a 64 percent Yes rate on the autonomy questions. A similar set of questions in RA-FIT Round 1 for 2010 had a Yes rate of 53 percent.

As might be expected, there is a significant difference on the question of autonomy between respondents with a ministry governance structure and those that self-identify as a semi-autonomous organization on the question of autonomy (Figure 5).

- Overall, semi-autonomous revenue administrations have an 87 percent Yes rate on the autonomy questions, versus a comparable rate of 47 percent for revenue administrations within a ministry of finance. The level of autonomy was rated higher for semi-autonomous administrations in every question, with percentage differences ranging from 62 points to 9 points.

- In terms of the major groupings of autonomy questions, the largest difference in the autonomy Yes rates is in the human resources area: 87 percent versus 37 percent (the first four characteristics in Figure 5).

- The most significant difference in all the autonomy questions is the ability to hire and fire staff: a 94 percent Yes rate for the semi-autonomous respondents versus 32 percent for those in a ministry.

A higher Yes rate for the semi-autonomous group is to be expected; however, the magnitude of the difference between the two groups is surprising. It will be interesting to expand the analysis on this issue in the next round (ISORA), which will include a significantly larger group of HICs, in which the autonomy rate for ministry administrations could be much higher than it was in the RA-FIT Round 2 group.

The ultimate test for autonomy, and to a certain extent for transparency, will be to determine whether higher levels of autonomy or transparency are related to higher levels of operational performance. Sample sizes for Round 2 are a bit low for this type of analysis, and data quality needs at least one more round of improvement.

Transparency

To increase the autonomy available to revenue administrations, it is necessary to reduce central agency public service controls. This is usually accomplished by increases in accountability, including reporting and transparency requirements. These accountability requirements have become more important to both types of revenue administrations, those in ministries and those that are semi-autonomous (in the latter case, management boards have taken a particular interest in accountability).

RA-FIT Round 2 includes seven Yes/No questions dealing generally with the subject of transparency in revenue administration. The responses for 2013 are summarized in Figure 6.

- Overall, semi-autonomous revenue administrations have an 86 percent Yes rate on the transparency questions versus a rate of 52 percent for revenue administrations within a ministry of finance.

- One of the more significant differences in the transparency questions is whether or not annual reports and strategic/business plans are published: The ministry structure administrations show a Yes rate of 50 percent, compared with a Yes rate in the low to mid-90s for the semi-autonomous

Figure 6. Transparency Responses Yes Rate per Question, 2013

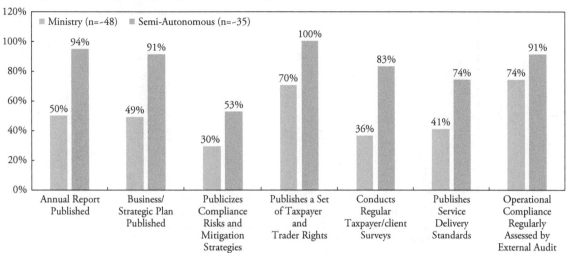

Figure 7. Tax - Cost of Collection, 2010 and 2013

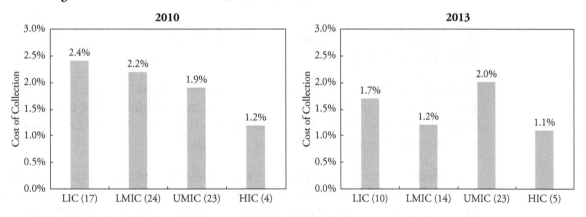

group. Many would consider the requirement to publish key documents such as annual reports and strategic plans a minimum level of transparency for purposes of public accountability.

Generally, it appears that transparency correlates well with autonomy, which is expected.

Budget

The 2015 edition of "Understanding Revenue Administration" (Lemgruber and others 2015) noted that the cost of collection is a frequently used indicator to measure the efficiency of revenue administration. This indicator is the ratio of the revenue collected to the total budget (operating and capital)

Figure 8. Tax Administration and Social Security Contributions

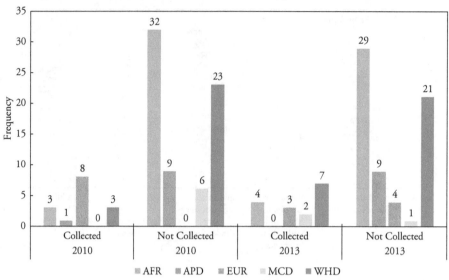

of the administration. All else being equal, reductions in this value indicate improvements in efficiency.

However, this indicator must be interpreted with extreme caution, because all things are rarely equal. Cost efficiency of a revenue administration is affected by many factors, which makes this indicator a risky one to use in cross-country cost comparisons (Lemgruber and others 2015).

A preliminary analysis from Round 1 showed that the administration cost, on average, tended to decrease for tax administrations from LICs through HICs. Possible explanations include the following: tax as a percentage of GDP generally increases across income groups (that is, from LICs to HICs), because many mature revenue administrations demonstrate a higher degree of professionalism, have a larger cadre of well-trained and highly skilled staff, have more advanced IT systems, and are in a better position to effectively curb tax avoidance and evasion. Figure 7 contrasts the costs of tax collection for 2010 with those for 2013.

In 2013 the trend was similar to that in 2010 except for UMICs, where costs of collection had increased slightly. LICs and LMICs, on the other hand, appear to have experienced noticeable improvements in the cost of collection over the three-year period. (Sample sizes for these groups were lower in 2013 than in 2010.)

Social Security Collections

In RA-FIT Round 1, some 82 percent of surveyed tax administrations indicated no social security contribution (SSC) collection responsibility for 2010. The model of combining tax and social security collection is more common in eastern Europe and seems to predominate in countries in which SSC revenues are an important source of revenue (PIT and SSC are significant tax sources in Europe). The similarities of the processes to administer taxes on labor income—namely, PIT and SSC, which are important revenue bases in advanced economies—may have been the catalyst for some of these countries having chosen to combine tax and social security collection functions. In this survey, most tax administrations that collect SSCs are in UMICs and HICs. Figure 8 compares the situation in 2010 with the 2013 results from Round 2.

RA-FIT Round 2 data showed that for 2013 some 80 percent of respondents indicated no SSC collection responsibility. While the responses vary between the two RA-FIT rounds—especially with respect to European (EUR) participants—African (AFR) and Latin and Central American, including the Caribbean (WHD) participants are largely similar, if not slightly expanded. Most noticeable is the increase in the number of WHD respondents reporting that they do collect social security contributions. (APD refers to administrations in the Asia Pacific Region, and MCD to those in the Middle East and Central Asia.)

Contracting Out

The first report in this series on "Understanding Revenue Administration" (Lemgruber and others 2015) commented on various outsourcing issues based on the RA-FIT Round 1 survey. Table 5 takes the same issues and compares the 2010 responses with those from 2013.

Table 5. Selected Data Relating to Contracting Out (Outsourcing)

	2010	2013
Number of countries engaged in some level of outsourcing	60	60
Of which outsourcing		
Collection and payment processing to banks	42%	48%
Debt collection	8%	15%
IT services	40%	43%
Taxpayer audit	2%	8%

Outsourcing services appears to be a growing trend in a number of areas, notably in taxpayer audit—from 2 percent to 8 percent over the three years surveyed. Based on 2013 results (Appendix Table 8 includes services not included in Round 1), the most common outsourced services continue to be training (67 percent of those engaged in outsourcing), cash/banking services (48 percent), and information technology (43 percent).

4 Staffing and Office Networks

The form on staffing and office networks had questions dealing with full-time equivalents for tax and customs (where integrated with tax) operations as well as administration and support. It also collected information on headquarters FTEs, tax and customs (where integrated with tax) FTEs by function, and tax administration FTEs across the entire office network (see Appendix Tables 9 through 11).

Tax Operations Functions

Respondents were given a definition of tax operations FTEs[1] and asked to break down these employees into four subgroups: (1) client account management (including taxpayer services); (2) audit, investigation, and other verification; (3) enforced debt collection; and (4) other. Table 6 displays this information by income group for 2013.[2]

- LICs invest the smallest share of human resources in audit and investigation. This is not surprising, as it has long been observed that LICs have the least developed audit staff and compliance risk management approaches. HICs, on the other hand, have about 40 percent of total resources in audit and verification, or 50 percent if enforced collection is included. These

---

[1]Tax operations FTEs refer to *taxpayer account management functions*—staff involved in taxpayer registration and other taxpayer services, tax file processing staff, payment including cashiers, and other staff who interact and provide taxpayer services and education; *audit, investigation, and other verification*—staff involved in audit, investigation, and other tasks involved with verification of taxpayer statements and claims, including the management of objections and appeals; *enforced debt collection and related functions*—staff who are directly involved in debt collection and enforcement; and *other tax operations functions*—any other staff who do not fit into the previous categories.

[2]Data from 2013 are used for analytical purposes in this section, as there is little difference between the 2013 data and the data for 2011 and 2012.

Table 6. Average Staff Distribution across Tax Operations by Income Group, 2013 **(Percentage)**

Income Group	Client Account Management Functions	Audit, Investigation, and Other Verification	Enforced Debt Collection and Related Functions	Other Tax Operations Functions
LICs (15)	32	23	19	26
LMICs (21)	29	36	12	23
UMICs (25)	31	34	14	21
HICs (8)	24	36	9	30
All Respondents (69)	**30**	**32**	**14**	**24**

Numbers in parentheses equal the average sample size for data supplied.

rules of thumb would appear to be borne out by the data, although the relatively small sample size for HICs reduces confidence in this conclusion. ISORA will add many more HICs to the data set for future analysis.

- HICs invest the smallest share of human resources in enforced collection. Again, the small sample size makes it difficult to extrapolate this conclusion.

Office Networks and Staff Distribution

Information was gathered on tax operations staff distributed across office networks by income group (Table 7). Similar data were requested in Round 1, but lack of definitions rendered the data of low quality.

While new definitions have led to better quality data, there still appears to be a problem with the distinction between regional and local offices. The problem appears particularly acute regarding LMICs, where a significantly higher percentage of staff are located in regional offices compared with local offices. This is exactly the opposite of what would be expected, as regional structures are normally smaller coordinating offices in many tax administrations. A further review of these data confirmed that many respondents did not apply the definition in this manner. Improved definitions for the ISORA round are expected to resolve this issue.

Tax Administration Staff Metrics

RA-FIT Round 1 analysis made a number of comments about the appropriate size of a revenue administration workforce, using three different measures for 2010: (1) staff ratios for population, (2) active labor force, and (3) PIT taxpayers. In Round 2, similar data were captured. Figure 9 shows the ratios

22

Figure 9. Tax Administration Staff Metrics

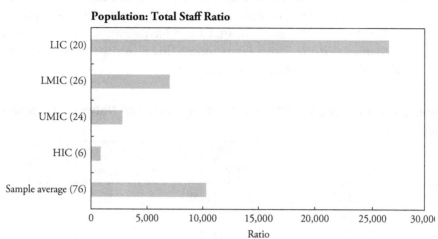

Population: Total Staff Ratio

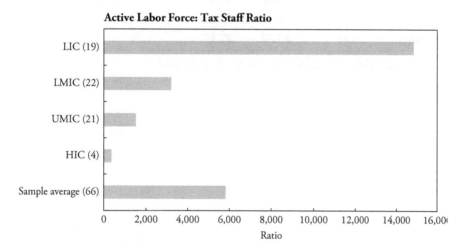

Active Labor Force: Tax Staff Ratio

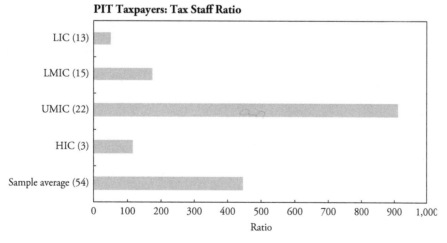

PIT Taxpayers: Tax Staff Ratio

of staff across the three measures for 2013. While not directly comparable to the 2010 data owing to differences in the makeup of the sample, the pattern remains broadly the same, in that LICs have many fewer staff covering the population and the active labor force. This result is reversed for PIT, where LIC staff cover fewer taxpayers on average.

Table 7. Average Tax Operations Staff Distributed across Office Network by Income Group, 2013 (Percentage)

Income Group	Headquarters	Regional Offices	Local Offices	Data Processing Centers	Service (Call) Centers	Other Offices
LICs (14)	32.38	21.12	38.20	1.09	0.16	7.05
LMICs (21)	38.90	41.21	15.14	0.35	2.70	1.70
UMICs (25)	33.87	25.69	31.65	4.75	1.44	2.60
HICs (8)	28.14	27.23	25.47	2.37	0.99	15.81
All respondents (68)	34.44	29.72	27.17	2.36	1.51	4.79

Numbers in parentheses equal the average sample size for data supplied.

CHAPTER

5 Taxpayer Segmentation

Administrations use segmentation of their taxpayer bases to varying degrees to manage their taxpayers, from both a compliance and a service perspective. The form on taxpayer segmentation covers some basic questions for tax administrations only. It includes questions about large taxpayer offices and simplified regimes for small taxpayers; thus, the emphasis is on size-based categorization of taxpayer segments (see Appendix Tables 12 through 16).

Large Taxpayer Office Results

The majority of respondents across the three years of Round 2 stated that they have an LTO, with over 84 percent answering Yes in 2013 compared to 77 percent for 2010 Round 1 results, and the number of countries with LTOs increased over the 2011–13 period. A majority in each of the income groups reported having LTOs (Figure 10). UMICs had the largest number of respondents without LTOs: 25 percent in 2013. These UMIC cases are, however, all small island nations in the Caribbean and Pacific, which is similar to Round 1 results.

The survey asked respondents to list the four main criteria for determining a large taxpayer. These free text data were examined and the criteria reported were categorized. The most common criterion by far was turnover—65 of 70 responses listed this as a segmentation criterion (Figure 11). This is to be expected, as size is the most common means of segmenting taxpayers, often into large, medium, and small groupings. The other categories are listed below, with industry or sector as the next most common criterion, followed by type of taxes paid. Other means of segmenting taxpayers, such as behavioral-risk-driven criteria, appear uncommon.

Figure 10. Large Taxpayer Office or Equivalent by Income Group—Frequency

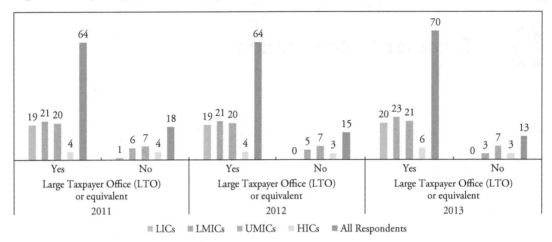

Figure 11. Large Taxpayer Office or Equivalent Criteria—All Respondents

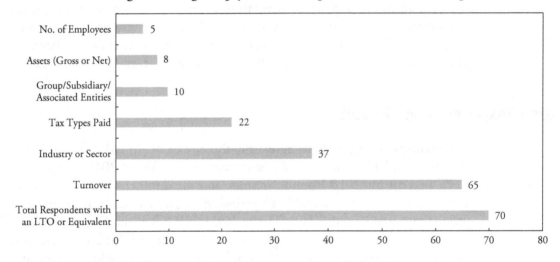

For those who indicated that they had an LTO, the survey asked several additional questions concerning staff, number and type of taxpayers managed by the LTO, and revenue attributable to managed taxpayers. The percentage of total active CIT taxpayers managed by the LTOs, varied widely across the income groups, but the trend overall seemed to be decreasing over the three years, particularly among LICs (Figure 12).

The percentage of staff allocated to work in LTOs doubled on average from 5 percent in Round 1 (2010) to 10 percent in Round 2. It remained fairly static over the three years 2011–13, suggesting a more accurate response in Round 2 (see Figure 13).

Figure 12. Large Taxpayer Office Metrics by Income Group—CIT Taxpayers
(Percentage of Total Active Corporate Income Taxpayers Managed by LTO)

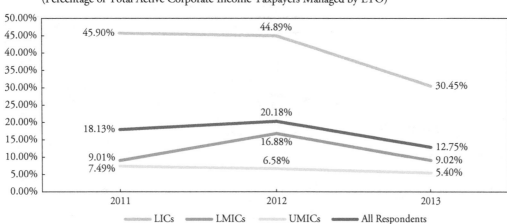

Figure 13. Large Taxpayer Office Metrics by Income Group—FTEs
(Percentage of Total Tax Operations FTEs in the LTO)

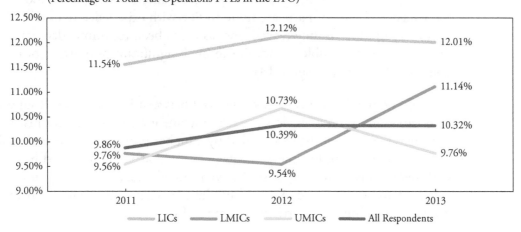

On the other hand, the ratio of CIT taxpayers to LTO staff FTEs has increased since Round 1 across the income groups, from 13:1 in 2010 to 18:1 in 2013. This could reflect a number of factors, including categorization changes resulting in more cases classified as large taxpayers, increasing numbers of large taxpayers in the case base, a reduction in overall or LTO staff numbers in LTOs/overall reduction in staff numbers, or combinations of all of these. The ratio would be a concern if LTOs are relatively understaffed and this trend continues, given the relative complexity of the cases that they manage.

In Round 1 the revenue attributable to LTOs was about 48 percent of the domestic tax revenue. In Round 2 responses the share rose to over 58 per-

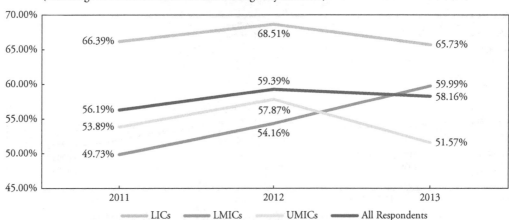

Figure 14. Large Taxpayer Office Metrics by Income Group—Domestic Revenue
(Percentage of Total Domestic Revenue Managed by the LTO)

cent in 2013, with increases between 2010 and 2013 seen in LICs (50 to about 66 percent), LMICs (45 to 60 percent), and UMICs (48 to about 53 percent). These estimates are more in line with experience than those in Round 1, and this finding is welcome, as it has been recommended generally that LTOs be responsible for administering a significant proportion of total domestic tax revenue (Figure 14).

Overall, the picture seems to have changed between Round 1 and Round 2, with variation in some respects between income groups. More administrations have LTOs, and they are staffed by a higher proportion of overall staff (double, on average), but the percentage of CIT taxpayers managed by these staff members is decreasing or static, even though taxpayer-to-staff ratios have increased and the revenue managed by the LTOs generally increased between Round 1 and Round 2, particularly among LICs.

Simplified Regime for Small Taxpayers

Small taxpayers present different challenges to administrations from a service and compliance perspective. They may be numerous and deal mostly in the cash or informal economy, but it is often worth registering them and managing them as efficiently as possible. To that end, many administrations have instituted small taxpayer regimes. In Round 1, slightly more than half of respondents had such a regime. By 2013, in Round 2, over two-thirds of the respondents (54 of 81) stated that they had some sort of regime. These regimes are proportionately more common in lower income groups (Figure 15).

Figure 15. Simplified Regimes for Small Taxpayers by Income Group—Frequency

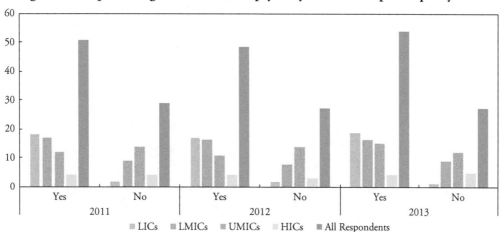

Figure 16. Simplified Regime Types for Small Taxpayers, 2013

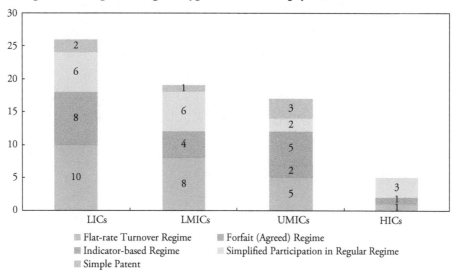

The survey asked an additional question on the type of regimes used. Flat-rate turnover regimes, *Forfait* and simplified participation are most common among lower income groups, with indicator-based regimes appearing among higher income groups (Figure 16). Respondents could select more than one option. The types of regimes offered are likely related to the types of economies in each income group and the varying capacity levels of the administrations.

6 Taxpayer Registration

Taxpayer registration is a critically important area for any tax administration—an efficient and effective registration function is the platform on which all other functions of the administration are built. Therefore, it is important for administrations to have an up-to-date and accurate sense of their case base and the activity status of their cases, as well as a reliable means of registering new taxpayers and recording their basic attributes. The form on taxpayer registration covers some basic questions for tax administrations only; the questions principally concern the main taxes: VAT, PIT, and CIT (see Appendix Tables 17 through 21).

VAT Registration

The first questions in this form concern whether administrations have a VAT and the thresholds applicable. In all income groups across all years surveyed (Figure 17), a large majority (over 90 percent in 2013) have a VAT. Not all respondents provided data for all three years.

The average threshold for VAT registration was $55,400 in 2013; it increased slightly over the three years of the survey. There is little difference in the threshold across income groups. Different administrations may have different motivations for getting taxpayers registered for VAT. In 2013, no other VAT thresholds were applicable to certain taxpayers in 75 percent of cases. Voluntary VAT registration was possible with more than 84 percent of respondents who provided data for 2013 (Figure 18).

Figure 17. National/Federal VAT by Income Group—Frequency

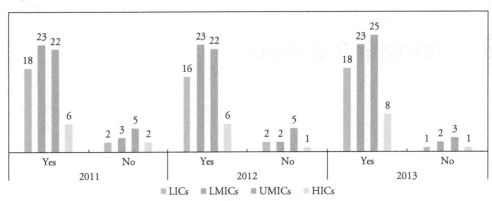

Figure 18. Voluntary VAT Registration by Income Group—Frequency

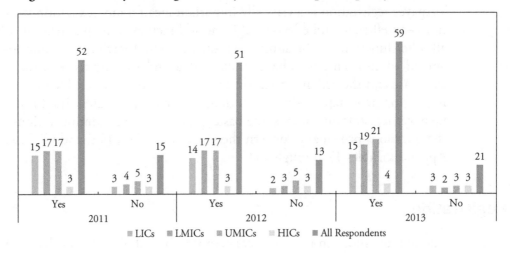

Taxpayer Activity Status

The next section of the form breaks down the registered taxpayers into "Total" and "Active" across PIT, CIT, VAT, sales tax, and excise tax. Obviously not all taxpayers on a register will be active at any one time; it is important to know the status of a taxpayer, so that they can be treated accordingly at the individual level but also so that planning can be informed by workflow and expected activity at the overall level. The responses give an overview of the distribution of the tax types among the income groups. PIT (the majority in all cases), CIT, employer PAYE, and VAT registrations make up the bulk of the taxpayer base across income groups, while sales and excise tax are relatively small by comparison. LMICs stand out as having fewer individual taxpayers on average as compared with the other income groups, and LICs have the fewest VAT and CIT (Figure 19) for 2013.

Figure 19. Distribution of Total Tax Register by Income Group, 2013

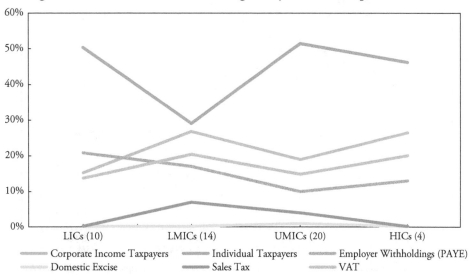

A large number of respondents, across income groups, had difficulty providing high-quality responses regarding the activity status of the taxpayers in their taxpayer base. For example, 16 countries provided the same figures for "Total" and "Active" for income tax (corporate and others) and VAT across all three years. Others could provide only one or the other.

Generally, as income levels increase, the proportions of active taxpayers on the register decrease across the tax types (Figure 20; Appendix Table 21). Factors affecting this include the age of the administration, the accuracy of the register, and the economic environment of the taxpayer base being managed.

The importance of the accuracy of the responses to this form—especially with regard to active taxpayers—is related to the return filing form, as the number of returns to be filed will be influenced by the number of active taxpayers on the register.

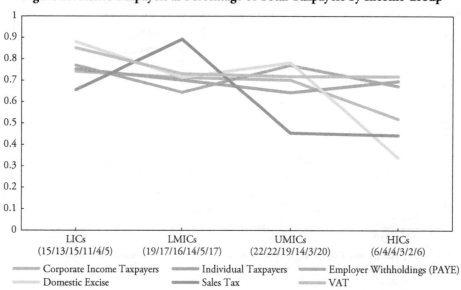

Figure 20. Active Taxpayers as Percentage of Total Taxpayers by Income Group

Note: Numbers in parentheses equal the average sample size for data supplied for each tax type, as per the tables in appendix.

7 Return Filing

Returns filing data are another key metric in measuring administration performance and taxpayer compliance. The questions on filing were split over two forms in the survey (VAT and Other Taxes) but are presented together in this paper. The core questions on these forms cover the basics, such as expected and actual returns, as well as late filers and electronic filers, and return types in the case of VAT (debit, credit, nil) (see Appendix Tables 22 through 27).

The first question in this section asked if there was a universal filing requirement for PIT (Figure 21). Over the three-year period the responses remained relatively stable, with the majority of administrations (66 percent in 2013) indicating that they had a universal filing requirement. Lower income groups mainly responded Yes, while UMICs were evenly split and a majority of HICs (albeit with a small sample size) said No.

Filing Rates

In Round 1 filing rates showed room for improvement, particularly for income taxes. The filing rates for VAT were on average better, for reasons such as filing frequency and the self-enforcing nature of VAT (through the input tax credits mechanism, with taxpayers looking for refunds). In Round 2, the results show a similar pattern.

Filing Rates—Corporate Income Tax

Corporate income tax filing rates were on average sitting at about 57 percent for all income groups in 2013. This was an improvement over 49 percent in 2010 but still leaves much to be desired. There was some variation in the

Figure 21. Personal Income Tax Universal Filing by Income Group—Frequency

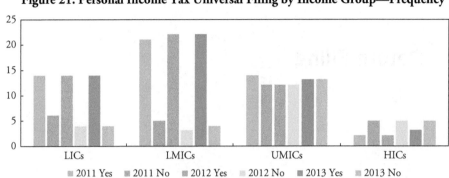

Figure 22. CIT On-Time Filing vs. Filing Six Months after Due Date

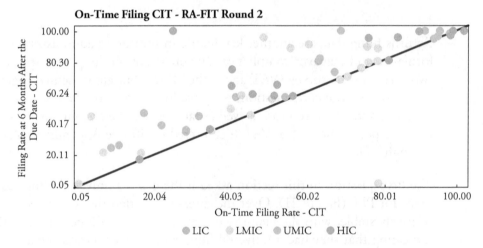

average in each income group. The improvement in filing rates six months after the due date also varied (Figures 22 and 23). In some cases, there was substantial improvement, suggesting the possibility of follow-up compliance work by the administrations, while in others no improvement was shown between the on-time filing rate and six months later. This may also reflect a data quality problem where data were not available for one or the other measure.

Filing Rates—Personal Income Tax

Personal income tax filing rates (determined by combining employee and self-employed categories in the survey) were on average 50 percent in 2013. This compares to 45 percent in 2010, which is an improvement but again shows room to maneuver upward, and not all income groups showed improvement across 2011–13 (Figure 24). As with CIT, there were a wide

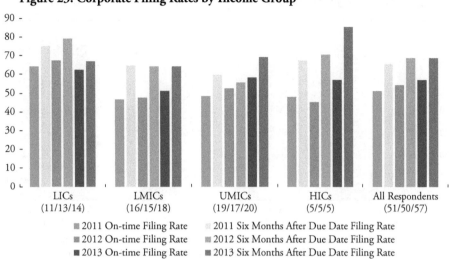

Figure 23. Corporate Filing Rates by Income Group

LICs (11/13/14) • LMICs (16/15/18) • UMICs (19/17/20) • HICs (5/5/5) • All Respondents (51/50/57)

■ 2011 On-time Filing Rate ■ 2011 Six Months After Due Date Filing Rate
■ 2012 On-time Filing Rate ■ 2012 Six Months After Due Date Filing Rate
■ 2013 On-time Filing Rate ■ 2013 Six Months After Due Date Filing Rate

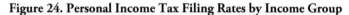

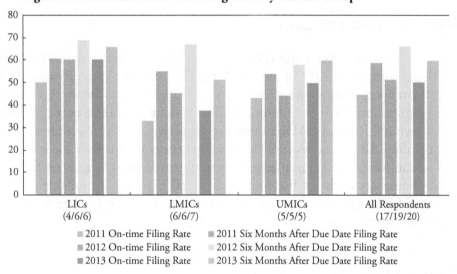

Figure 24. Personal Income Tax Filing Rates by Income Group

LICs (4/6/6) • LMICs (6/6/7) • UMICs (5/5/5) • All Respondents (17/19/20)

■ 2011 On-time Filing Rate ■ 2011 Six Months After Due Date Filing Rate
■ 2012 On-time Filing Rate ■ 2012 Six Months After Due Date Filing Rate
■ 2013 On-time Filing Rate ■ 2013 Six Months After Due Date Filing Rate

range of values around the average, with some lower-income countries reporting very bad on-time filing rates. There were fewer responses for PIT than for CIT, because PIT was not applicable or data were not available. The filing rates six months after the due date were on average about 10 percent higher in 2013, once again suggesting room for improvement. These rates are likely to be a mix of compliance issues and inaccurate estimates of expected returns driven by issues with the register. It is also possible that many expected PIT filers could be dealt with in a more efficient manner by, for example, removing the requirement to file a detailed return. The data from HICs were insufficient to provide a useful average.

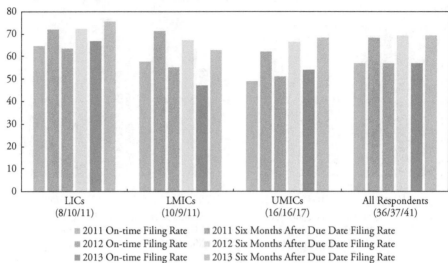

Figure 25. Employer Withholding (PAYE) Filing Rates by Income Group

Filing Rates—Pay As You Earn

Employer withholding (PAYE) filing rates were better than PIT rates, with an average in 2013 of almost 57 percent on time, rising to almost 70 percent on average filing rate after six months (Figure 25). The average on-time and six-month-later filing rates for LMICs show a decrease over the three years, while LICs and UMICs show overall improvements. As with all the return filing data, there was a wide range of results within each income group, so caution is needed in interpreting and comparing averages. (A full range of summary statistics, including means and medians, is available through the RA-FIT Data Portal http://data.rafit.org.) Once again, data from HICs were insufficient to provide a useful average.

Filing Rates—Value Added Tax

VAT on-time filing rates were better than those for other taxes in Round 1 (69 percent), and this remained the case in Round 2, with the average rate almost unchanged at slightly more than 68 percent on average in 2013 (Figure 26). Six-months-later filing averaged about 80 percent in 2013, the best of all the taxes surveyed. Across all income groups, the rates were above 60 percent on average, which is not the case with the other taxes. The frequency of filing VAT returns (for example, monthly, quarterly) was requested in the survey, but for the sake of simplicity the results are reported in the aggregate for all VAT filer types.

Figure 26. VAT Filing Rates by Income Group

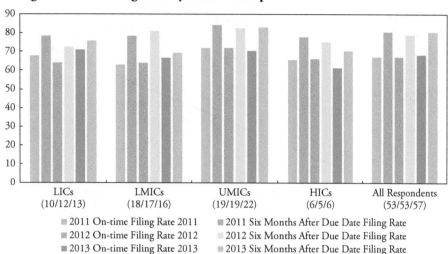

LICs (10/12/13)   LMICs (18/17/16)   UMICs (19/19/22)   HICs (6/5/6)   All Respondents (53/53/57)

■ 2011 On-time Filing Rate 2011   ■ 2011 Six Months After Due Date Filing Rate
■ 2012 On-time Filing Rate 2012   ■ 2012 Six Months After Due Date Filing Rate
■ 2013 On-time Filing Rate 2013   ■ 2013 Six Months After Due Date Filing Rate

Figure 27. VAT On-Time Filing, 2011–13

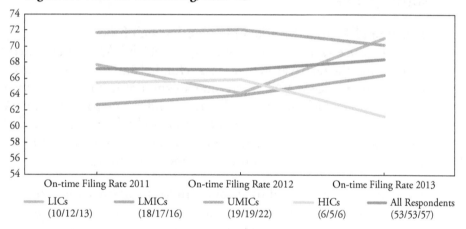

On-time Filing Rate 2011   On-time Filing Rate 2012   On-time Filing Rate 2013

— LICs (10/12/13)   — LMICs (18/17/16)   — UMICs (19/19/22)   — HICs (6/5/6)   — All Respondents (53/53/57)

The income groups show mixed trends in overall average VAT on-time filing rates over the three years in Round 2 (Figure 27). LICs and LMICs improved most over the period, while HICs showed a downward trend, albeit with a small sample. UMICs had the best rates, particularly for filing six months after the due date. Overall, the rates marginally improved between 2011 and 2013.

When the data are viewed as a scatter plot, it is clear that while there are a range of values, the majority of cases are in the higher ranges of filing rates, both on time and six months after the due date, concentrating in the top right corner of the plot (Figure 28). This is the zone in which administrations should aim to have their filing rates.

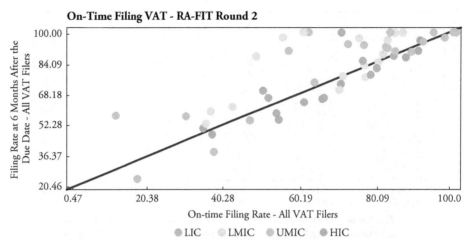

Figure 28. VAT On-Time Filing vs. Filing Six Months after Due Date

VAT Filing—Return Types

Like Round 1, Round 2 asked for a breakdown of the VAT return types. There are three types: (1) credit returns, in which VAT inputs exceed VAT outputs and the taxpayer may make a refund claim; (2) debit returns, in which outputs exceed VAT inputs and an amount is due to be paid; and (3) nil returns, in which inputs equal outputs and the taxpayer owes no VAT. Round 1 found a large proportion of credit and nil returns; in Round 2, the results were similar. Debit returns make up about 50 percent of the returns, with credit and nil returns constituting the other 50 percent.

When the data are viewed by income group, a pattern similar to that in Round 1 emerges, with increasing average proportions of debit returns and decreasing proportions of credit returns as income levels rise. The nil returns also decrease slightly as income levels increase (Figure 29). This pattern is consistent across the three years and thus likely to be robust. For LICs—with the highest relative proportion of credit returns but with lower refund rates—this is an issue for monitoring and concern. Are VAT regimes operating correctly in LICs? Are risks inherent in credit returns and nil returns being adequately assessed and addressed?

Figure 30 shows VAT refund rates for LICs, LMICs, and UMICs. The LICs generally show the lowest average VAT refunds paid out or offset against other tax liabilities as a percentage of total value claimed. However, over the three-year period there was some improvement in both LICs and LMICs. If VAT refunds as a percentage of gross VAT collections are compared with total net VAT as a percentage of total revenue, it can be seen that VAT refunds in LICs remain a challenge in that proportionately much less VAT is being refunded on average in LICs than in the other income groups.

Figure 29. Categories (Debit, Credit, Nil) of VAT Returns by Income Group

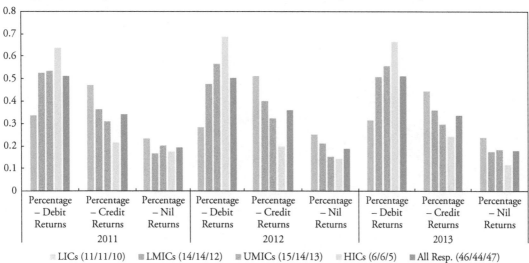

Figure 30. VAT Refunds Paid Out or Offset against Other Tax Liabilities
(Percentage of Total Value Claimed)

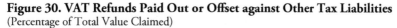

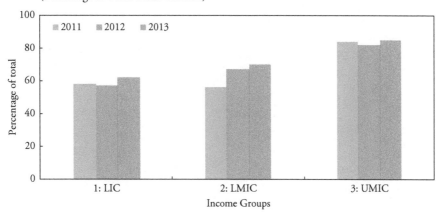

8 Taxpayer Service

The taxpayer service form was a first step in covering some new ground not covered by Round 1; namely, some aspects of how tax administrations provide services to their taxpayers. The questions cover the channels used to receive queries from taxpayers (see Appendix Table 28).

The channels listed include the main methods taxpayers use to communicate with their tax administration: in-person interaction, telephone, and written communication. The summary data presented here are from 2013, the most recent data available, but it is possible to see shifts in the country-level data as new channels are introduced and taxpayers start using them.

Overall, the most commonly used channel is in-person or face-to-face communication, averaging over 46 percent (Figure 31). This is a costly channel to maintain and provide compared with other channels. It is followed by call center and written communication (about 17 percent and 15 percent, respectively), which can also involve relatively high costs. Use of the cheapest options (while not always appropriate) is minimal by comparison; for example, use of IVR[1] is reported at less than 4 percent. This suggests that for many administrations there is considerable potential to move at least some queries from more costly channels to less costly ones as part of an informed taxpayer service development strategy.

When the survey results are split into income groups, some immediate differences are apparent. The LICs have a relatively high average proportion of costly channel activity on average. Written communication, which includes hardcopy letters and forms, makes up over a third (36 percent) of all queries. This may reflect the nature of the administrations and their

---

[1]Interactive voice response (IVR) is a technology that allows a computer to interact with, in this case, a taxpayer through the use of voice and dual-tone multifrequency tones input via the telephone's keypad.

Figure 31. Queries by Channel by Income Group

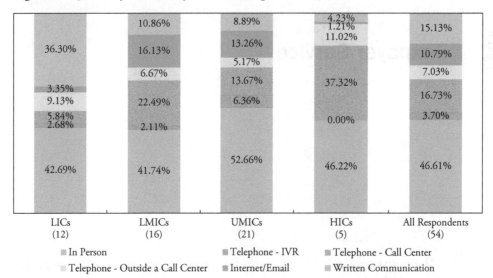

practices, as well as taxpayer access to telephones and the Internet in 2013. It might be possible in the future to shift some of these queries to online or telephone options. In-person contacts are the most used channel across all income groups: LICs and LMICs have similar proportions (42 percent and 43 percent, respectively), and UMICs have, at 42/3 percent, interestingly this rises for UMICs to almost 53 percent, and it is the biggest channel across all income groups. LMICs show a higher proportional use of the Internet and email than LICs (over 16 percent to over 3 percent) and greater use of call centers (22.5 percent versus about 6 percent), perhaps suggesting a path LICs could take to reduce costs. The HIC sample is too small to draw robust conclusions, but it is worth noting that these cases have the highest average proportion of queries handled by a call center, at over 37 percent.

Data on service channels should be relatively easy to record and access within a tax administration, but only 54 respondents supplied data for this form for 2013. This suggests room for immediate improvement, as this area is a basic one from the perspective of cost, manpower planning, and ensuring that voluntary compliance is supported and developed. Finally, it is worth reiterating that a mix of channels will generally still be required to service different taxpayer types/segments and requirements, but costs can be reduced by better targeting of lower-cost options to the appropriate taxpayer types and their needs.

9 Tax Arrears

The response to questions on tax arrears in Round 1 was very poor, with only 17 respondents providing full data. This was a cause for concern, as arrears and debt management are core functions of any tax administration and basic data on this function should be immediately at hand. The situation greatly improved in Round 2, with 66 respondents providing data, although the quality and completeness of these data is questionable. Not all of the data are reported here (see Appendix Tables 29 through 32).

The overall average for tax arrears in dispute rose over the Round 2 three-year period to nearly 15 percent in 2013. The percentage varied across income levels, with LICs and HICs seeing downward trends into 2013, and LMICs and UMICs showing upward trends (Figure 32). It would be worth investigating the causes of these trends; for example, increases might be caused by backlogs of cases piling up over time or more taxpayers availing themselves of dispute resolution processes.

Often debts must be written off as irrecoverable; for example, owing to company liquidation or the death of a taxpayer. Again the trend here is mixed among income groups. LICs and HICs saw upward trends into 2013, and LMICs and UMICs showed downward trends; thus the average evens out to about 12 percent to 13 percent (Figure 33).

Recoverable arrears were estimated on average to be 73 percent in 2013, with a range of 67 percent in LICs to over 85 percent in LMICs. This measure was on average fairly stable over the 2011–13 period (Figure 34).

Growth in arrears as a percentage of total collections was most marked in the LIC countries between 2011 and 2012, although the rate of growth slowed between 2012 and 2013 as it did on average overall, dropping from 37 percent to about 25 percent (Figure 35). This downward trend is welcome

Figure 32. Tax Arrears in Dispute
(Percentage of Total Arrears at Year's End)

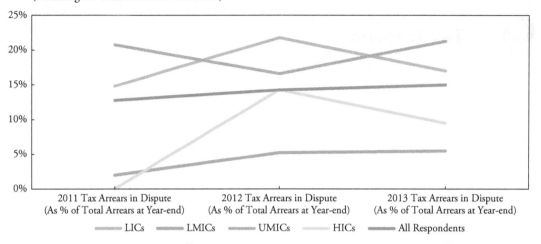

Figure 33. Tax Arrears Deemed Irrecoverable
(Percentage of Total Arrears at Year's End)

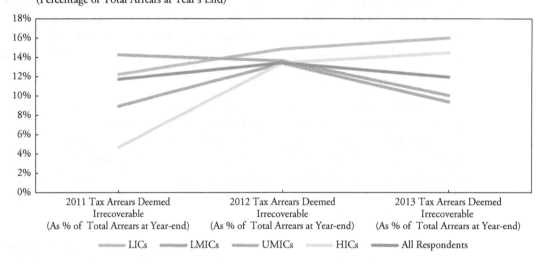

and should be monitored on an ongoing basis. LMICs and UMICs showed upward trends that should also be monitored.

Arrears as a percentage of collections is often used as a measure of performance; for example, in TADAT, a ratio below 10 percent is required to receive an "A" grade for that dimension. In Round 2, the results showed an increase in this measure, on average, as income levels increased (Figure 36). Only LICs scored an "A" by the TADAT measure across the years. This measure needs to be considered with some caution, as LICs tend to have lower filing rates, so tax arrears may be unrecorded. This means that tax arrears in LICs are often significantly understated.

Figure 34. Recoverable Arrears
(Percentage of Total Arrears at Year's End)

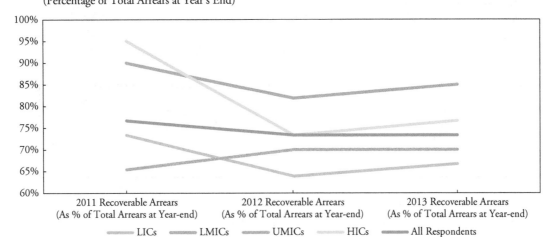

Figure 35. Growth in Tax Arrears by Income Group

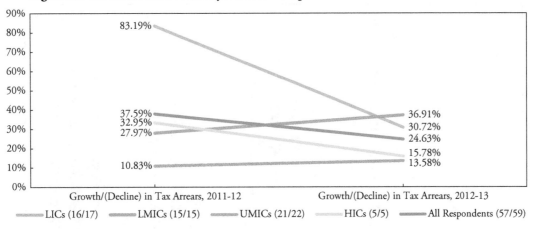

Figure 36. Total Tax Arrears as Percentage of Total Collections by Income Group

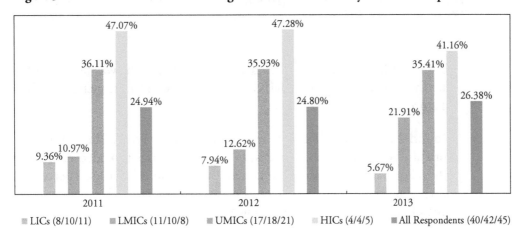

Figure 37. Trend in Total Tax Arrears as Percentage of Total Collections by Income Group

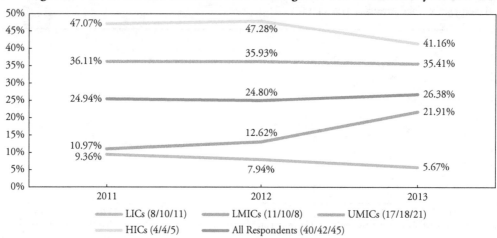

Figure 38. Average Percentage of Tax Arrears Older than 12 Months

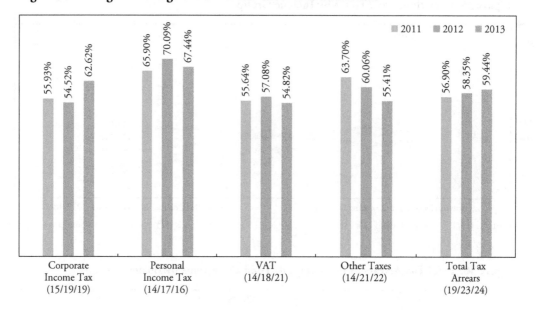

The trend in arrears as a percentage of total collections was fairly stable over the three years, except for LMICs, which saw an average increase in 2013 (Figure 37).

Round 2 also asked about arrears for different tax types. The response rate for this section was poor; for example, only 24 cases provided data for 2013. Overall, total average arrears for these cases stood at nearly 60 percent in 2013 (Figure 38), which—given the risk mentioned earlier— should be an area of concern and ongoing monitoring over time.

10 Tax Verification/Audit

The tax verification/audit form asked some basic questions about verification/audit within administrations, including types of interventions, volume, and the value of additional assessments (see Appendix Tables 33 and 34).

Audit and other interventions are core activities in a tax administration. A properly functioning audit program—ideally driven mainly by risk-based selection—is a primary way of ensuring taxpayer compliance and fairness in the tax system.

Verification includes a variety of actions that vary in scope and intensity. This form split the actions into the following types, defined on the form for clarity as follows:

- Comprehensive audit: "an action that is usually in depth; covers multiple taxes and numerous issues and tax years; and is mostly carried out at the premises of the taxpayer"
- Issue-oriented audit (divided into income tax, VAT, PAYE, and other types): "an action usually focused on specific issues, taxes, or tax years, and normally carried out at the premises of the taxpayer"
- Desk audit: "an action usually resulting from an in-office review of information returned by the taxpayer and normally takes the form of further written or telephonic enquiries"
- Other verification action: "any additional measures taken by the authorities, usually encompassing high-volume automated checks such as income/document cross-matching"

For each of these types, the form asked for the number of taxpayers and total additional assessment values. There was also a section asking for a breakdown of these data for large taxpayers, but these data are not covered in this report. It is possible that some administrations, owing to deficiencies in their case

Figure 39. Audit Types as Percentage of Total Audits by Income Group (Number), 2013

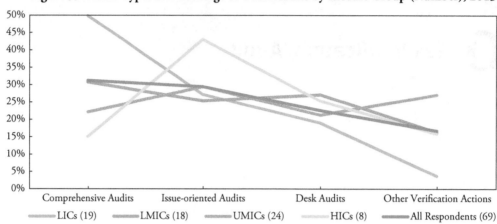

management systems, were unable to determine the intervention types and provide a breakdown and so combined the data for all types into one category. There were no questions in Round 2 on the "hit rate" of verification actions, but this topic will appear in the next round (ISORA).

Taking 2013 as a basis for comparison (HICs are not present in sufficient numbers in 2011 or 2012), the mix of intervention types varies across income levels. For example, LICs show the highest relative average proportion of comprehensive audits at almost 50 percent of the intervention mix (a decrease from 57 percent in 2011). They also show the lowest proportion of "other verification actions." This suggests that LICs emphasize more costly and more intensive interventions compared with higher income groups, where the mix is more evenly spread (Figure 39). The situation is similar to that found in 2010 in Round 1.

The value of additional assessments raised follows a similar pattern with, on average, most yield for LICs coming from comprehensive audits and very little from other verification actions, although this is low across all income groups (Figure 40).

The average number of cases percentage and value percentage of the respective totals can be combined in one plot. Figure 41 shows that the majority of the action and results occur with comprehensive and issue-oriented audits, suggesting that there is considerable scope across most income groups for expanding the use of different audit types and perhaps reducing costs associated with intensive intervention types for both the administration and taxpayers.

Figure 40. Audit Types as Percentage of Total Audits by Income Group (Value), 2013

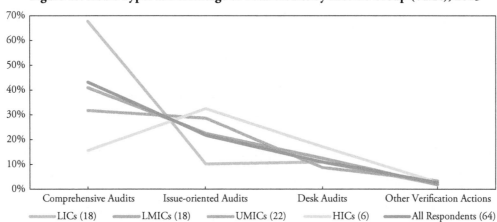

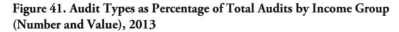

Figure 41. Audit Types as Percentage of Total Audits by Income Group
(Number and Value), 2013

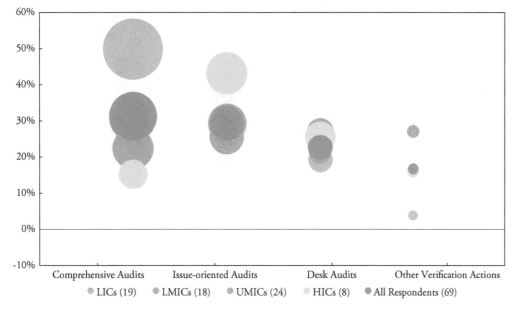

51

11 Dispute Resolution

This last form in the survey asks some volumetric questions concerning disputes (objections) and litigation (appeals) (see Appendix Table 35).

As in Round 1, the response rate to this form was poor, with only a third of participants providing data. This response is of concern, as the dispute resolution procedures available to taxpayers are an important assurance of fair treatment as well as a mechanism to challenge potential errors caused at the administrative level or as the result of some intervention or action by the administration.

The data provided have been summarized to an overall level, as an income group breakdown is not meaningful. Only data on litigation had sufficient responses. In absolute terms, the age of the appeals is not changing greatly for those that responded; however, there was an increase from 2012 to 2013 for cases that are one to five years old compared with cases less than a year old. If this trend were to persist, it would be a cause of concern (Figure 42).

However, the greatest concern is that so many respondents either do not have a dispute resolution process that they can report on or failed to provide data on this important area of their administration.

Figure 42. Litigation (Appeals) Cases by Age (Number)

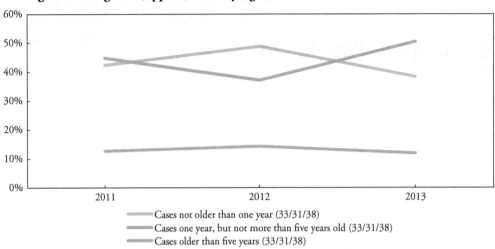

12 General Conclusions

The second round of RA-FIT was a step beyond the first round, and the next step is the collaborative initiative known as ISORA, the International Survey on Revenue Administration. Round 2 was limited in some respects, owing to its geographic bias, lack of representation from higher-income countries, and some data quality limitations. Nevertheless, much can be said in summary about the countries that did provide data. Countries can, upon registration, access their data at http://data.rafit.org for their own purposes and comparative analyses.

Overall, there seems to be wide variation across the income groups in many operational areas, but there is variation within income groups as well, so some caution is required when using averages for comparisons. The institutional arrangements and the staff and office profiles vary enough to suggest that the sample is diverse and represents various types of administrations, at least among the LICs, LMICs, and UMICs. Correlating attributes of administrations with targets of interest is possible, but it may be prudent to wait for ISORA data before drawing any overall conclusions.

What Round 2 does provide is a series of baselines across a number of key areas for tax administration. In all cases (for example, with return filing, service channel mix, arrears management, and audit intervention mix) there appears to be room for improvement within and across all income groups. The results also show some improvement in trends over the three years surveyed. Countries should take stock of where they are at a point in time and among their peers, and be aware of any emerging trends.

Many participants had difficulty answering all the questions on the Round 2 survey. This is surprising given how straightforward many of the questions were, particularly as much of this information should be closely monitored by senior management on an ongoing basis. Administrations can use Round

2 and ISORA as guides to how they could set up their own performance management systems.

Lessons were learned in conducting Round 2, and many of these have been carried forward into the development of ISORA, which aims to create a representative, stable, and comprehensive set of measures over time.

References

BoardSource: Nonprofit Governance Index 2012. Data Report 1 CEO Survey of BoardSource Members. BoardSource, Washington, DC

International Monetary Fund, (IMF). 2010. *Revenue Administration: Autonomy in Tax Administration and the Revenue Authority Model.* IMF Technical Note, Washington, DC.

Lemgruber, A, Masters, A and Cleary, D. 2015. Understanding Revenue Administration. An Initial Data Analysis Using the Revenue Administration Fiscal Information Tool. Fiscal Affairs Department departmental paper series. IMF, Washington, DC.

Appendix Tables

Institutional Arrangements

Appendix Table 1. Type of Institutional Arrangement by Income Group—Frequency

	2013			
Income Group	Single Directorate in Ministry	Multiple Directorates in Ministry	Semi-autonomous Body	Semi-autonomous Body with a Board
LICs	6	2	0	9
LMICs	9	3	4	7
UMICs	12	4	6	5
HICs	4	2	3	0
All Respondents	**31**	**11**	**13**	**21**

Appendix Table 2. Semi-autonomous Revenue Bodies with Boards—Board Type and Size (All)

	2011	2012	2013
Decision-Making Board (No.)	15	15	16
Advisory Board (No.)	5	5	5
Total Semi-autonomous Bodies with Boards (No.)	20	20	21
Average No. of Board Members (Mean)	8	8	8
Average No. of Private Sector Board Members (Mean)	4	4	4

Appendix Table 3. Management of Tax and Customs by Income Group—Frequency

Income Group	2011		2012		2013	
	Tax and Customs Separate	Tax and Customs Co-managed	Tax and Customs Separate	Tax and Customs Co-managed	Tax and Customs Separate	Tax and Customs Co-managed
LICs	9	8	8	8	8	9
LMICs	12	9	13	9	14	9
UMICs	15	12	13	12	16	11
HICs	5	5	4	5	4	5
All Respondents	**41**	**34**	**38**	**34**	**42**	**34**

Appendix Table 4a. Degree of Autonomy by Income Group—Frequency (All)

Income Group	2013													
	Design Own Internal Structure		Set Level of Staff Remuneration		Establish Staffing Levels and Mix		Hire and Fire Staff		Exercise Discretion over Operating Expenditure		Exercise Discretion over Capital Expenditure		Establish Performance Standards	
	Yes	No	Yes	No	Yes	No	Yes	No	Yes	No	Yes	No	Yes	No
LICs	11	10	6	14	13	8	11	10	12	9	9	12	18	3
LMICs	19	6	10	16	14	11	15	11	15	10	16	9	25	0
UMICs	19	8	12	15	24	3	17	10	19	9	16	12	26	1
HICs	6	2	2	6	4	4	4	4	8	0	6	2	8	0
All Respondents	**55**	**26**	**30**	**51**	**55**	**26**	**47**	**35**	**54**	**28**	**47**	**35**	**77**	**4**

Appendix Table 4b. Degree of Autonomy by Income Group—Frequency (Tax Only)

| Income Group | 2013 | | | | | | | | | | | | | |
| | Design Own Internal Structure | | Set Level of Staff Remuneration | | Establish Staffing Levels and Mix | | Hire and Fire Staff | | Exercise Discretion over Operating Expenditure | | Exercise Discretion over Capital Expenditure | | Establish Performance Standards | |
	Yes	No	Yes	No	Yes	No	Yes	No	Yes	No	Yes	No	Yes	No
LICs	3	9	1	10	5	7	3	9	5	7	2	10	9	3
LMICs	10	5	5	10	8	7	7	8	6	9	7	8	15	0
UMICs	11	5	6	10	13	3	9	7	11	6	10	7	16	0
HICs	3	1	1	3	2	2	3	1	4	0	4	0	4	0
All Respondents	27	20	13	33	28	19	22	25	26	22	23	25	44	3

Appendix Table 4c. Degree of Autonomy by Income Group—Frequency (Tax and Customs)

| Income Group | 2013 | | | | | | | | | | | | | |
| | Design Own Internal Structure | | Set Level of Staff Remuneration | | Establish Staffing Levels and Mix | | Hire and Fire Staff | | Exercise Discretion over Operating Expenditure | | Exercise Discretion over Capital Expenditure | | Establish Performance Standards | |
	Yes	No	Yes	No	Yes	No	Yes	No	Yes	No	Yes	No	Yes	No
LICs	8	1	5	4	8	1	8	1	7	2	7	2	9	0
LMICs	9	1	5	6	6	4	8	3	9	1	9	1	10	0
UMICs	8	3	6	5	11	0	8	3	8	3	6	5	10	1
HICs	3	1	1	3	2	2	1	3	4	0	2	2	4	0
All Respondents	28	6	17	18	27	7	25	10	28	6	24	10	33	1

Appendix Table 5a. Degree of Transparency by Income Group—Frequency (All)

| Income Group | 2013 | | | | | | | | | | | | | |
| | Publishes Annual Report | | Publishes Strategic/Business Plan | | Publicizes Compliance Risks and Mitigation Strategies | | Publishes a Set of Taxpayer Rights | | Conducts Regular Taxpayer Surveys | | Publishes Service Delivery Standards | | Is Externally Audited | |
	Yes	No	Yes	No	Yes	No	Yes	No	Yes	No	Yes	No	Yes	No
LICs	11	10	13	8	11	10	18	3	11	10	13	6	14	5
LMICs	20	6	20	5	11	14	20	5	13	12	15	10	19	6
UMICs	21	7	19	9	8	20	24	4	16	12	13	15	25	3
HICs	5	4	3	6	2	6	6	2	6	3	4	5	7	1
All Respondents	57	27	55	28	32	50	68	14	46	37	45	36	65	15

Appendix Table 5b. Degree of Transparency by Income Group—Frequency (Tax Only)

| Income Group | 2013 | | | | | | | | | | | | | |
| | Publishes Annual Report | | Publishes Strategic/Business Plan | | Publicizes Compliance Risks and Mitigation Strategies | | Publishes a Set of Taxpayer Rights | | Conducts Regular Taxpayer Surveys | | Publishes Service Delivery Standards | | Is Externally Audited | |
	Yes	No	Yes	No	Yes	No	Yes	No	Yes	No	Yes	No	Yes	No
LICs	4	8	6	6	5	7	9	3	4	8	6	4	7	3
LMICs	11	4	11	4	6	9	12	3	5	10	9	6	12	3
UMICs	11	6	10	7	6	11	15	2	10	7	9	8	14	3
HICs	3	1	2	2	1	3	4	0	3	1	2	2	4	0
All Respondents	29	19	29	19	18	30	40	8	22	26	26	20	37	9

Appendix Table 5c. Degree of Transparency by Income Group—Frequency (Tax and Customs)

| | 2013 | | | | | | | | | | | | | |
| | Publishes Annual Report | | Publishes Strategic/Business Plan | | Publicizes Compliance Risks and Mitigation Strategies | | Publishes a Set of Taxpayer Rights | | Conducts Regular Taxpayer Surveys | | Publishes Service Delivery Standards | | Is Externally Audited | |
Income Group	Yes	No	Yes	No	Yes	No	Yes	No	Yes	No	Yes	No	Yes	No
LICs	7	2	7	2	6	3	9	0	7	2	7	2	7	2
LMICs	9	2	9	1	5	5	8	2	8	2	6	4	7	3
UMICs	10	1	9	2	2	9	9	2	6	5	4	7	11	0
HICs	2	3	1	4	1	3	2	2	3	2	2	3	3	1
All Respondents	28	8	26	9	14	20	28	6	24	11	19	16	28	6

Appendix Table 6. Cost of Administration by Income Group

Income Group	2011		2012		2013	
	Recurrent Cost of Administration (Excludes Capital Costs)	Total Cost of Administration (Recurrent and Capital Costs)	Recurrent Cost of Administration (Excludes Capital Costs)	Total Cost of Administration (Recurrent and Capital Costs)	Recurrent Cost of Administration (Excludes Capital Costs)	Total Cost of Administration (Recurrent and Capital Costs)
Revenue Administrations (tax and customs co-managed in a single administration)						
LICs (5)	1.98%	2.11%	2.57%	2.70%	2.06%	2.33%
LMICs (4)	1	1	1	1	1	1
UMICs (6)	1.53%	1.57%	1.51%	1.57%	1.58%	1.64%
HICs (0)	-	-	-	-	-	-
All Respondents (15)	**1.67%**	**1.74%**	**1.82%**	**1.91%**	**1.80%**	**1.94%**
Tax Administrations (tax only administration)						
LICs (5)	0.90%	1.09%	0.77%	0.89%	0.87%	1.01%
LMICs (10)	0.66%	0.75%	0.75%	0.84%	0.80%	0.89%
UMICs (17)	1.94%	2.02%	1.80%	1.92%	2.02%	2.08%
HICs (5)	1.52%	1.54%	1.07%	1.08%	1.11%	1.13%
All Respondents (37)	**1.37%**	**1.46%**	**1.25%**	**1.34%**	**1.39%**	**1.47%**

Numbers in parentheses equal the average sample size for data supplied.
[1]Fewer than five respondents.

Appendix Table 7. Outsourced Services by Income Group—Frequency

Income Group	2011		2012		2013	
	Yes	No	Yes	No	Yes	No
LICs	14	6	13	6	15	6
LMICs	18	7	19	5	19	5
UMICs	21	6	19	7	21	6
HICs	4	4	4	3	5	3
All Respondents	57	23	55	21	60	20

Appendix Table 8. Main Types of Outsourced Services by Income Group—Frequency

Income Group	2013						
	Analytical Services (Technical/Policy)	Cash/ Banking Services	Client Services	Debt Collection Services	IT Services	Taxpayer Audit	Training
LICs	5	10	0	3	4	0	11
LMICs	6	8	1	4	6	2	12
UMICs	4	10	3	1	13	2	13
HICs	2	1	2	1	3	1	4
All Respondents	17	29	6	9	26	5	40

Staffing and Office Network

Appendix Table 9. Average Staffing—Support, Operations, and Headquarters by Income Group

	2011				2012				2013			
Income Group	HR, Admin, and Other Support (% of Total FTEs)	Tax Operations (% of Total FTEs)	Customs Operations (% of Total FTEs)	Headquarters (% of Total FTEs)[1]	HR, Admin, and Other Support (% of Total FTEs)	Tax Operations (% of Total FTEs)	Customs Operations (% of Total FTEs)	Headquarters (% of Total FTEs)[1]	HR, Admin, and Other Support (% of Total FTEs)	Tax Operations (% of Total FTEs)	Customs Operations (% of Total FTEs)	Headquarters (% of Total FTEs)[1]
Revenue Administrations (tax and customs co-managed in a single administration)												
LICs (7)	33%	32%	35%	25%	32%	33%	35%	26%	33%	34%	33%	24%
LMICs (6)	33%	35%	32%	43%	28%	39%	33%	38%	29%	39%	32%	32%
UMICs (6)	17%	51%	32%	18%	18%	52%	30%	18%	19%	51%	30%	18%
HICs (1)	2	2	2	2	2	2	2	2	2	2	2	2
All Respondents (20)	**28%**	**39%**	**33%**	**27%**	**26%**	**41%**	**33%**	**26%**	**26%**	**43%**	**31%**	**22%**
Tax Administrations (tax only administration)												
LICs (13)	28%	72%	-	34%	27%	73%	-	34%	22%	78%	-	36%
LMICs (19)	29%	71%	-	52%	27%	73%	-	44%	27%	73%	-	49%
UMICs (20)	25%	75%	-	54%	23%	77%	-	46%	23%	77%	-	49%
HICs (7)	14%	86%	-	44%	16%	84%	-	49%	17%	83%	-	56%
All Respondents (59)	**26%**	**74%**	**-**	**47%**	**25%**	**75%**	**-**	**43%**	**23%**	**77%**	**-**	**47%**

Numbers in parentheses equal the average sample size for data supplied.

[1]Include both support and operations headquarters staff.

[2]Fewer than five respondents.

Appendix Table 10. Average Staff Distribution across Tax Operations by Income Group

Income Group	2011				2012				2013			
	Client Account Management Functions	Audit, Investigation, and Other Verification	Enforced Debt Collection and Related Functions	Other Tax Operations Functions	Client Account Management Functions	Audit, Investigation, and Other Verification	Enforced Debt Collection and Related Functions	Other Tax Operations Functions	Client Account Management Functions	Audit, Investigation, and Other Verification	Enforced Debt Collection and Related Functions	Other Tax Operations Functions
LICs (15)	32%	24%	18%	26%	31%	24%	19%	26%	32%	23%	19%	26%
LMICs (21)	28%	37%	13%	22%	30%	35%	13%	22%	29%	36%	12%	23%
UMICs (25)	31%	34%	16%	19%	33%	32%	15%	20%	31%	34%	14%	21%
HICs (8)	20%	33%	5%	41%	22%	34%	7%	37%	24%	36%	9%	30%
All Resp. (69)	29%	32%	15%	24%	31%	31%	14%	23%	30%	32%	14%	24%

Numbers in parentheses equal the average sample size for data supplied.

Appendix Table 11. Average Tax Operations Staff Distributed across Office Network by Income Group

Income Group	2013					
	Headquarters	Regional Offices	Local/ Branch Offices	National/ Regional Data Processing Centers	National/ Regional Service Centers (including Call Centers)	Other Offices
LICs (14)	32.38%	21.12%	38.20%	1.09%	0.16%	7.05%
LMICs (21)	38.90%	41.21%	15.14%	0.35%	2.70%	1.70%
UMICs (25)	33.87%	25.69%	31.65%	4.75%	1.44%	2.60%
HICs (8)	28.14%	27.23%	25.47%	2.37%	0.99%	15.81%
All Respondents (68)	34.44%	29.72%	27.17%	2.36%	1.51%	4.79%

Numbers in parentheses equal the average sample size for data supplied.

Appendix Table 12. Large Taxpayer Office or Equivalent by Income Group—Frequency

Income Group	2011		2012		2013	
	Yes	No	Yes	No	Yes	No
LICs	19	1	19	0	20	0
LMICs	21	6	21	5	23	3
UMICs	20	7	20	7	21	7
HICs	4	4	4	3	6	3
All Respondents	64	18	64	15	70	13

Taxpayer Segmentation

Appendix Table 13. Large Taxpayer Office or Equivalent Criteria—All Respondents

2013	
LTO Criteria Used by Five or More Respondents	Number
Total Respondents with an LTO or Equivalent	70
Turnover	65
Industry or Sector	37
Taxes Paid	22
Group/Subsidiary/Associated Entities	10
Assets (Gross or Net)	8
No. of Employees	5

Appendix Table 14. Large Taxpayer Office Metrics by Income Group Means

Income Group	Percentage of Total Active Corporate Income Taxpayers Managed by LTO	Percentage of Total Tax Operations FTEs in the LTO	Ratio of LTO CIT Payers to LTO FTEs[1]	Percentage of Total Domestic Revenue Managed by the LTO
2011				
LICs (14/15/14/13)	45.90%	11.54%	18:1	66.39%
LMICs (15/17/18/13)	9.01%	9.76%	19:1	49.73%
UMICs (17/17/20/16)	7.49%	9.56%	20:1	53.89%
HICs (4/3/3/1)	[2]	[2]	[2]	[2]
All Respondents (50/52/55/43)	**18.13**	**9.86%**	**20:1**	**56.19%**
2012				
LICs (15/17/15/13)	44.89%	12.12%	15:1	68.51%
LMICs (14/18/16/15)	16.88%	9.54%	21:1	54.16%
UMICs (18/18/20/17)	6.58%	10.73%	17:1	57.87%
HICs (4/3/3/1)	[2]	[2]	[2]	[2]
All Respondents (51/56/54/46)	**20.18%**	**10.39%**	**18:1**	**59.39%**
2013				
LICs (15/15/16/12)	30.45%	12.01%	23:1	65.73%
LMICs (17/21/21/16)	9.02%	11.14%	17:1	59.99%
UMICs (19/18/20/17)	5.40%	9.76%	13:1	51.57%
HICs (5/5/5/1)	0.26%	3.85%	20:1	[2]
All Respondents (56/59/62/46)	**12.75%**	**10.32%**	**18:1**	**58.16%**

Numbers in parentheses equal the average sample size for data supplied for each metric.
[1]Rounded to nearest FTE.
[2]Fewer than five respondents.

Appendix Table 15. Simplified Regimes for Small Taxpayers by Income Group—Frequency

Income Group	2011		2012		2013	
	Yes	No	Yes	No	Yes	No
LICs	18	2	17	2	19	1
LMICs	17	9	16	8	16	9
UMICs	12	14	11	14	15	12
HICs	4	4	4	3	4	5
All Respondents	**51**	**29**	**48**	**27**	**54**	**27**

69

Appendix Table 16. Types of Simplified Regimes for Small Taxpayers by Income Group—
Frequency

Income Group	Flat-Rate Turnover Regime	*Forfait* (Agreed) Regime	Indicator-Based Regime	Simplified Participation in Regular Regime	Simple Patent
2011					
LICs	7	8	1	7	4
LMICs	8	5	0	9	1
UMICs	5	2	6	1	2
HICs	1	1	1	1	1
All Respondents	**21**	**15**	**7**	**20**	**7**
2012					
LICs	7	8	0	7	3
LMICs	8	4	0	6	1
UMICs	4	2	6	0	2
HICs	1	0	1	3	0
All Respondents	**20**	**14**	**7**	**16**	**6**
2013					
LICs	10	8	0	6	2
LMICs	8	4	0	6	1
UMICs	5	2	5	2	3
HICs	1	0	1	3	0
All Respondents	**24**	**14**	**6**	**17**	**6**

[1] Fewer than five respondents.

Taxpayer Registration

Appendix Table 17. National/Federal VAT by Income Group—Frequency

Income Group	2011		2012		2013	
	Yes	No	Yes	No	Yes	No
LICs	18	2	16	2	18	1
LMICs	23	3	23	2	23	2
UMICs	22	5	22	5	25	3
HICs	6	2	6	1	8	1
All Respondents	**69**	**12**	**67**	**10**	**74**	**7**

Appendix Table 18. Average General VAT Threshold by Income Group—US Dollars

Income Group	2011	2012	2013
LICs (16/16/17)	$56,059	$58,711	$58,747
LMICs (15/17/18)	$50,867	$52,342	$52,175
UMICs (14/14/15)	$48,455	$48,119	$54,030
HICs (4/4/5)	[1]	[1]	$60,051
All Respondents (49/51/55)	$50,477	$51,735	$55,428

[1]Fewer than five respondents.

Appendix Table 19. Voluntary VAT Registration by Income Group—Frequency

Income Group	2011 Yes	2011 No	2012 Yes	2012 No	2013 Yes	2013 No
LICs	15	3	14	2	15	3
LMICs	17	4	17	3	19	2
UMICs	17	5	17	5	21	3
HICs	3	3	3	3	4	3
All Respondents	52	15	51	13	59	11

Appendix Table 20. Distribution of Total Tax Register by Income Group

Income Group	Corporate Income Taxpayers	Individual Taxpayers	Employer Withholding (PAYE)	Domestic Excise	Sales Tax	VAT
LICs (10)	15.02%	50.32%	20.70%	0.20%	0.26%	13.49%
LMICs (14)	26.73%	28.94%	17.11%	0.22%	6.73%	20.27%
UMICs (20)	18.85%	51.25%	9.87%	1.07%	4.08%	14.88%
HICs (4)	[1]	[1]	[1]	[1]	[1]	[1]
All Respondents (48)	20.97%	44.11%	14.50%	0.55%	3.71%	16.15%

Numbers in parentheses equal the average sample size for data supplied.

[1]Fewer than five respondents.

Appendix Table 21. Active Taxpayers as Percentage of Total Taxpayers by Income Group

| Income Group | 2013 | | | | | |
	Corporate Income Taxpayers	Individual Taxpayers	Employer Withholding (PAYE)	Domestic Excise	Sales Tax	VAT
LICs (15/13/15/11/4/5)	74.21%	75.26%	76.91%	87.61%	[1]	85.07%
LMICs (19/17/16/14/5/17)	71.49%	69.81%	64.33%	70.96%	89.05%	72.77%
UMICs (22/22/19/14/3/20)	70.22%	64.09%	76.85%	77.96%	[1]	71.52%
HICs (6/4/4/3/2/6)	51.83%	[1]	[1]	[1]	[1]	71.81%
All Respondents (62/56/54/42/14/58)	**69.80%**	**68.80%**	**72.44%**	**74.99%**	**66.59%**	**75.42%**

Numbers in parentheses equal the average sample size for data supplied for each tax type.

[1]Fewer than five respondents.

Return Filing

Appendix Table 22. Personal Income Tax Universal Filing by Income Group—Frequency

| Income Group | 2011 | | 2012 | | 2013 | |
	Yes	No	Yes	No	Yes	No
LICs	14	6	14	4	14	4
LMICs	21	5	22	3	22	4
UMICs	14	12	12	12	13	13
HICs	2	5	2	5	3	5
All Respondents	**51**	**28**	**50**	**24**	**52**	**26**

Appendix Table 23. Corporate Filing Rates by Income Group

Income Group	2011 On-Time Filing Rate	2011 Six Months after Due Date Filing Rate	2012 On-Time Filing Rate	2012 Six Months after Due Date Filing Rate	2013 On-Time Filing Rate	2013 Six Months after Due Date Filing Rate
LICs (11/13/14)	64.07%	75.22%	67.32%	79.05%	62.34%	66.90%
LMICs (16/15/18)	46.49%	64.75%	47.55%	64.22%	51.08%	64.08%
UMICs (19/17/20)	48.33%	59.68%	52.70%	55.64%	58.28%	69.36%
HICs (5/5/5)	47.84%	67.57%	45.27%	70.62%	56.85%	85.47%
All Respondents (51/50/57)	**51.10%**	**65.38%**	**54.21%**	**68.84%**	**56.88%**	**68.53%**

Numbers in parentheses equal the average sample size for data supplied for each year.

Appendix Table 24. Personal Income Tax Filing Rates by Income Group

Income Group	2011 On-Time Filing Rate	2011 Six Months after Due Date Filing Rate	2012 On-Time Filing Rate	2012 Six Months after Due Date Filing Rate	2013 On-Time Filing Rate	2013 Six Months after Due Date Filing Rate
LICs (10/11/11)	49.92%	60.68%	60.19%	68.66%	60.15%	65.59%
LMICs (12/13/15)	32.88%	54.97%	45.13%	66.86%	37.59%	51.16%
UMICs (17/15/16)	43.18%	53.64%	44.29%	58.05%	49.85%	59.75%
HICs (3/3/4)	[1]	[1]	[1]	[1]	[1]	[1]
All Respondents (42/42/46)	**44.47%**	**58.68%**	**51.07%**	**66.19%**	**50.08%**	**59.72%**

Numbers in parentheses equal the average sample size for data supplied for each year.
[1]Fewer than five respondents.

Appendix Table 25. Employer Withholding (PAYE) Filing Rates by Income Group

Income Group	2011		2012		2013	
	On-Time Filing Rate	Six Months after Due Date Filing Rate	On-Time Filing Rate	Six Months after Due Date Filing Rate	On-Time Filing Rate	Six Months after Due Date Filing Rate
LICs (8/10/11)	64.74%	71.87%	63.51%	72.41%	66.65%	75.44%
LMICs (10/9/11)	57.83%	71.21%	55.01%	67.02%	46.98%	62.89%
UMICs (16/16/17)	49.03%	62.22%	50.99%	66.51%	54.02%	68.13%
HICs (2/2/2)	[1]	[1]	[1]	[1]	[1]	[1]
All Respondents (36/37/41)	56.94%	68.14%	57.14%	69.23%	56.98%	69.50%

Numbers in parentheses equal the average sample size for data supplied for each year.
[1]Fewer than five respondents.

Appendix Table 26. VAT Filing Rates by Income Group

Income Group	2011		2012		2013	
	On-Time Filing Rate	Six Months after Due Date Filing Rate	On-Time Filing Rate	Six Months after Due Date Filing Rate	On-Time Filing Rate	Six Months after Due Date Filing Rate
LICs (10/12/13)	67.67%	78.51%	64.16%	72.47%	71.02%	75.74%
LMICs (18/17/16)	62.70%	78.47%	63.93%	80.87%	66.42%	69.03%
UMICs (19/19/22)	71.66%	83.89%	72.09%	82.50%	70.19%	83.19%
HICs (6/5/6)	65.48%	77.80%	65.85%	75.14%	61.28%	70.57%
All Respondents (53/53/57)	67.17%	80.35%	67.09%	79.01%	68.38%	80.13%

Numbers in parentheses equal the average sample size for data supplied for each year.

Appendix Table 27. Categories (Debit, Credit, Nil) of VAT Returns by Income Group

Income Group	2011			2012			2013		
	Percentage – Debit Returns	Percentage – Credit Returns	Percentage – Nil Returns	Percentage – Debit Returns	Percentage – Credit Returns	Percentage – Nil Returns	Percentage – Debit Returns	Percentage – Credit Returns	Percentage – Nil Returns
LICs (11/11/10)	33.71%	47.36%	23.14%	28.17%	51.32%	25.07%	31.58%	44.54%	23.88%
LMICs (14/14/12)	52.74%	36.54%	16.45%	47.59%	40.01%	21.05%	50.64%	35.72%	17.73%
UMICs (15/14/13)	53.62%	30.94%	20.2%	56.6%	32.47%	15.45%	55.46%	29.85%	18.64%
HICs (6/6/5)	63.85%	21.46%	17.62%	68.49%	19.83%	14.6%	66.38%	24.07%	11.46%
All Resp. (46/44/47)	50.98%	34.08%	19.35%	50.21%	35.91%	19.04%	51.02%	33.55%	17.93%

Numbers in parentheses equal the average sample size for data supplied for each year.

Taxpayer Service

Appendix Table 28. Queries by Channel by Income Group

Income Group	In Person	Telephone – IVR	Telephone – Call Center	Telephone – Outside a Call Center	Internet/ Email	Written Communication
LICs (12)	42.69%	2.68%	5.84%	9.13%	3.35%	36.30%
LMICs (16)	41.74%	2.11%	22.49%	6.67%	16.13%	10.86%
UMICs (21)	52.66%	6.36%	13.67%	5.17%	13.26%	8.89%
HICs (5)	46.22%	0.00%	37.32%	11.02%	1.21%	4.23%
All Respondents (54)	46.61%	3.70%	16.73%	7.03%	10.79%	15.13%

Numbers in parentheses equal the average sample size for data supplied.

Tax Arrears

Appendix Table 29. Tax Arrears by Income Group (Percentage of Total Arrears at Year's End)

Income Group	Tax Arrears in Dispute	Tax Arrears Deemed Irrecoverable	Recoverable Arrears
2011			
LICs (18)	14.76%	12.24%	73.00%
LMICs (16)	1.90%	8.95%	89.15%
UMICs (23)	20.71%	14.26%	65.03%
HICs (5)	0.00%	4.71%	95.29%
All Respondents (61)	**12.66%**	**11.73%**	**75.61%**
2012			
LICs (19)	21.65%	14.86%	63.49%
LMICs (15)	5.23%	13.39%	81.38%
UMICs (22)	16.56%	13.62%	69.81%
HICs (5)	14.24%	13.44%	72.32%
All Respondents (60)	**14.24%**	**13.44%**	**72.32%**
2013			
LICs (20)	16.92%	15.97%	67.12%
LMICs (16)	5.46%	9.41%	85.13%
UMICs (23)	21.13%	10.06%	68.82%
HICs (8)	9.36%	14.45%	76.19%
All Respondents (66)	**14.87%**	**11.97%**	**73.16%**

Numbers in parentheses equal the average sample size for data supplied.

Appendix Table 30. Growth in Tax Arrears by Income Group

Income Group	2012 Growth/(Decline) in Tax Arrears, 2011–12	2013 Growth/(Decline) in Tax Arrears, 2012–13
LICs (16/17)	83.19%	30.72%
LMICs (15/15)	27.97%	36.91%
UMICs (21/22)	10.83%	13.58%
HICs (5/5)	32.95%	15.78%
All Respondents (57/59)	**37.59%**	**24.63%**

Numbers in parentheses equal the average sample size for data supplied.

Appendix Table 31. Total Tax Arrears as Percentage of Total Collections by Income Group

Income Group	2011	2012	2013
LICs (8/10/11)	9.36%	7.94%	5.67%
LMICs (11/10/8)	10.97%	12.62%	21.91%
UMICs (17/18/21)	36.11%	35.93%	35.41%
HICs (4/4/5)	[1]	[1]	41.16%
All Respondents (40/42/45)	24.94%	24.80%	26.38%

Numbers in parentheses equal the average sample size for data supplied for each year.
[1]Fewer than five respondents.

Appendix Table 32. Average Percentage of Tax Arrears Older than 12 Months

Tax Type – All Respondents[1]	2011	2012	2013
Corporate Income Tax (15/19/19)	55.93%	54.52%	62.62%
Personal Income Tax (14/17/16)	65.90%	70.09%	67.44%
VAT (14/18/21)	55.64%	57.08%	54.82%
Other Taxes (14/21/22)	63.70%	60.06%	55.41%
Total Tax Arrears (19/23/24)	56.90%	58.35%	59.44%

Numbers in parentheses equal the average sample size for data supplied for each year.
[1]Limited data, not meaningful to present by income group.

Verification and Audit

Appendix Table 33. Audit Types as Percentage of Total Audits by Income Group (Number)

Income Group	Comprehensive Audits	Issue-Oriented Audits	Desk Audits	Other Verification Actions
2011				
LICs (16)	57.13%	20.95%	20.88%	1.03%
LMICs (19)	30.54%	27.46%	26.77%	15.23%
UMICs (22)	25.26%	29.77%	18.63%	26.34%
HICs (3)	[1]	[1]	[1]	[1]
All Respondents (60)	**34.41%**	**25.29%**	**23.41%**	**16.89%**
2012				
LICs (18)	55.77%	20.42%	20.26%	3.54%
LMICs (18)	26.76%	34.10%	24.86%	14.29%
UMICs (21)	20.12%	32.99%	17.54%	29.35%
HICs (4)	[1]	[1]	[1]	[1]
All Respondents (61)	**31.51%**	**29.20%**	**21.84%**	**17.45%**
2013				
LICs (19)	49.77%	27.05%	19.29%	3.89%
LMICs (18)	30.85%	25.56%	27.11%	16.48%
UMICs (24)	22.33%	29.31%	21.19%	27.16%
HICs (8)	15.20%	43.22%	25.68%	15.89%
All Respondents (69)	**31.28%**	**29.32%**	**22.73%**	**16.66%**

Note: Numbers in parentheses represent the number of respondents.

[1]Fewer than five respondents.

Appendix Table 34. Audit Types as Percentage of Total Audits by Income Group (Value)

Income Group	Comprehensive Audits	Issue-Oriented Audits	Desk Audits	Other Verification Actions
2011				
LICs (15)	62.16%	11.98%	13.63%	0.25%
LMICs (20)	40.45%	18.13%	16.69%	6.61%
UMICs (20)	47.18%	20.77%	9.43%	1.84%
HICs (4)	[1]	[1]	[1]	[1]
All Respondents (59)	**46.94%**	**17.76%**	**14.22%**	**3.34%**
2012				
LICs (17)	67.16%	10.66%	10.99%	0.52%
LMICs (18)	35.22%	25.07%	12.41%	2.23%
UMICs (19)	36.86%	25.47%	7.68%	4.53%
HICs (3)	[1]	[1]	[1]	[1]
All Respondents (57)	**44.91%**	**21.17%**	**9.97%**	**2.79%**
2013				
LICs (18)	67.71%	9.87%	10.77%	1.77%
LMICs (18)	41.01%	22.50%	12.57%	1.42%
UMICs (22)	31.59%	28.33%	8.76%	3.00%
HICs (6)	15.53%	32.53%	16.86%	2.56%
All Respondents (64)	**42.89%**	**21.89%**	**11.16%**	**2.17%**

Note: Numbers in parentheses represent the number of respondents.

[1]Fewer than five respondents.

Dispute Resolution

Appendix Table 35. Litigation (Appeals) Cases by Age (Number)

Litigation (Appeal) Cases – All Respondents[1]	2011	2012	2013
Cases less than 1 year old (33/31/38)	42.38%	48.49%	38.24%
Cases 1 to 5 years old (33/31/38)	44.85%	37.03%	49.99%
Cases more than 5 years old (33/31/38)	12.77%	14.48%	11.77%

Numbers in parentheses equal the average sample size for data supplied for each year.

[1]Limited data, not meaningful to present by income group.